LIES, LEGENDS & LORE OF THE SAN JUANS

(and a few true tales)

BY ROGER HENN

Western Reflections, Inc.

Library of Congress Catalog Number: 99-61618

ISBN 1-890437-29-8

Designed by Kim Weinstein, ARBOGAST DESIGNS

PUBLISHED BY:
Western Reflections Publishing Co.
P.O. Box 1647
Montrose, CO 81402
USA

E-Mail westref@montrose.net
www.westernreflectionspub.com

CONTENTS 🌿

PREFACE 🌿

"Lies, Legends and Lore" may seem a most peculiar or even twisted subject and title. Not really. Western history has been inescapably bound with lies and lore and legends. The San Juans of yesterday are a part of the western history that so fascinates not only those of America but also history buffs in England, Germany, and Japan.

Unfortunately too many of today's historians are engaged in debunking the lore involved with the history and the personalities of the West. They laugh at stories that have been handed down man-to-man, and mother-to-child over many generations. "These tales cannot possibly be true history," they say, "because there is no contemporary written or printed account that says this is so." So they happily write their history replete with footnotes, based upon scrubbed and cleaned-up family typewritten or printed histories that make Grandfather a paragon of virtue instead of the lovable, carousing and pleasure-loving man he once was — the man Grandmother loved, perhaps for his human faults as much as for fine attributes. No wonder so many of our youth are turned off by history. Give me the story that is told so well you are never sure when the truth stops and the great lie begins ......

CHAPTER I

THE GREAT BULL STORY

Many of the charming memories of my hometown of Ouray, Colorado are of the wild animals who seem to feel at home in our small city. There was a weasel who frequented our yard trying to get into the chicken coops. When winter came he was a gorgeous white (ermine). Snowshoe rabbits, white in the winter and brown in the summer, fattened themselves out in the grass and flowers while staying quiet so they wouldn't be seen. A red fox would occasionally raid our chicken yard. In the summer the chipmunks scurried busily in and out of the rock clefts.

But elk and deer, in those far off days near the turn of the century, had been hunted to near extinction by the prospectors who needed them to fill out their limited diets since they spent weeks and months seeking the mineral wealth they so seldom found.

As the mountains surrounding the town grew whiter and whiter with their mantel of snow, the animals moved from their higher ranges closer and closer to town.

Every winter evening the mountain sheep came leaping down the cliffsides to feed upon the bales of hay and the oats scattered along the railroad tracks near the town's depot. As far as I know this movement of the bighorns into human habitation was unique. While the sheep never became truly tame, they did become bold enough to challenge the small narrow gauge locomotives for "track rights" as they grazed on the feed that had been provided.

Like many of the charming customs of Ouray, the feeding of the mountain sheep was thoughtlessly discontinued; the sheep stopped visiting the city and their numbers drastically decreased. A few are still reported three miles below town and up Cutler Creek, but you have to be lucky to see them.

Another bit of uniqueness that the townspeople foolishly banished were the stately elk who at one time stalked up and down the streets, grazing on the sweet peas, peonies, and other vegetables in the gardens. Occasionally they posed for appropriate pictures in

front of the Elks Club (BPOE 492) on Main Street. The elk originally were a herd of six turned loose on the Amphitheater hillside in
the early 1920s. To be sure that they prospered, the city fathers
provided bales of hay and blocks of salt on the hillside. And they
did prosper! The cows left each spring to calf but returned each fall
with their new offspring. The old bulls never took occasion to leave
but settled comfortably into the town.

One favorite story is of five-year-old Martha McCullough who
was headed to a friend's home when, in crossing the bridge over
Portland Creek, she met head on with one of the great bulls. They
stopped and eyed each other. Then little Martha stomped her foot,
pointed her finger and told the great bull to turn around and go away.
The bull meekly did exactly as ordered.

A visiting minister, holding evening services at the Presbyterian
church, had brought two of his sons with him to enjoy the hot springs
pool and the drive from Delta. The service was interrupted by the
youngest boy screaming as he ran down the small church aisle. It
turned out he had stepped outside for a moment and came nose-to-
nose with one of the great bulls who was trying to see what was
going on inside the church.

Now this was in the days long before clothes dryers had been
invented. In that day clothes, after being washed, were hung out on
long wire lines that ran through pulleys on an endless line — one
pulley attached to the porch and the other to a convenient tree or
power pole some distance away. Some of the clothes lines were
utilized by housewives much closer to the ground; some very short
poles were even embedded in the ground. One of the elk roaming
through the yard might entangle a clothesline in his huge rack of
antlers, and as he wandered on his way the line of clothes streamed
after him. Usually a screaming housewife, swinging a threatening
broom, was following.

Grandmother lived with us, as was the expected family make-
up of that day. She was an early riser, and she usually built the fire
in the kitchen stove, set the oatmeal to boiling, and when the copper
clothes boiler was hot enough, boiled the Monday clothes wash.
She had a way with animals, and it soon became a daily occurrence
for one of the old bulls to pay a visit to her early in the morning.
Grandmother would call to the old bull, who would with great dig-

nity, reach his great neck across the porch railing to accept a slice of bread or a cup of uncooked oatmeal.

He became so much of a pet that Grandmother determined to put him to useful work. Of course she was familiar with the stories that the other woman used to tell at Ladies Aid of how their clothes had been dragged through mud by an elk whose antlers had become entangled in a clothes line. So on Monday morning when the clothes had finished boiling in the copper boiler and had been rung out through the hand wringer, Grandmother would go out on the porch and call her friend the elk. When the old bull responded she would arrange various towels and old clothes on his antlers, and off he would parade waving these items from his great rack. Half an hour later he would return with dried clothes and would be rewarded with an extra slice of bread, this one doctored with butter and brown sugar.

An elk roams Ouray with someone's underwear on its antlers. Was it put there on purpose? — COURTESY OF CARL COCKLE

CHAPTER 2 🌿

THE LIGHTNING STRUCK LOST MINE

Great ranches now spread across the valley of Cow Creek: Sleeping Ute, Chimney Rock, and others. Some have their own private jet landing strips. Their ranch houses are pretentious, spreading to tens of thousands of square feet. Cow Creek and its valley is greatly different from what it was like in the nineteenth century.

One early map calls Cow Creek, Bache Creek, which was the Spanish word for buffalo. It is also a term for cow. Could it have been possible that early Spanish explorers found the valley filled with grazing buffalo? There is one old, old building in Cow Creek that has a buffalo skull mounted over the door. Could it be that the skull might have been found nearby? The Spanish name suggests that Cow Creek was known to their trappers, miners, or explorers far earlier than we have acknowledged. We do know that the Escalante explorers reached the Uncompahgre at about the present-day location of Colona in 1776.

When the Ute reservation was moved to Colona, Cow Creek became the grazing grounds for the Ute cattle herds. Chief Ouray and his key sub chiefs were working to change the Utes from hunters to cattle raisers — a change Ouray recognized would be necessary if the Utes were to survive in the white man's world. If the Utes had another ten years in the Uncompahgre Valley before their expulsion, they might well have become successful agrarians.

My story of the lost mine of this Cow Creek country must begin with the first white man we have record of exploring it. Charlie Hall came to the San Juans with the ill-fated Baker parties. Having no success in finding placer gold in Baker's Park near present-day Silverton, Hall and two companions left to look at the Uncompahgre Valley in 1861. In the bowl that is today Ouray they found no gold in their panning so they proceeded down the stream, panning as they went. Like others of the Baker parties they watched where their feet walked looking for evidence of free gold; if they had raised their eyes, they would have seen gold and silver veins all around them.

Free gold, which can be collected by panning, is almost non-existent in the San Juans. Going downstream they encountered the recently abandoned camp of the Doc Arnold party that had spent the winter of 1860-61 a mile south of present-day Ridgway. The Arnold party was headed for Baker's Park and the hub-bub there but got lost and ended up in the Uncompahgre Valley trapped for the winter by heavy snow. Although they did find some gold, when spring came they left to travel on to the exciting Baker camp which had always been their goal.

Charlie and his two friends continued down the river to the junction with Cow Creek. Running out of food they headed up Cow Creek hoping to find a shortcut back to Baker's Park. Thus they became the first white men of record to have entered Cow Creek. Starving, they were so anxious to get back that they did no prospecting. In the years that followed Cow Creek remained unprospected.

And so we turn to our tale of the lost mine. First, however, much confusion exists in histories of Ouray as to two men named Long. As one of these is the center of our story we need to clarify this confusion. Robert F. Long was one of the group of thirteen men to first winter in Ouray. Long is first recorded as coming into the San Juans in early spring of 1875. With his small party he brought a number of wagons from Del Norte and started up Stony Pass, but the remaining heavy snow made it impossible to bring wagons over the pass. The wagons and supplies were left at Lost Trail Camp with a packer named Frank Blackledge who used Lost Trail as his headquarters. Long and his associates struggled up through the snow and then down to Cunningham Gulch and Howardsville. When the snow melted Long returned to Lost Trail, but to his dismay found the wagons burned and the valuable supplies missing. Blackledge had a number of conflicting stories, but Long never recovered the missing supplies.

Long worked his way up to Mineral Point (which with grandiose ideas was calling itself Mineral City) and joined a party of men setting out to explore the Uncompahgre. The story of this exploration is told in Chapter 32. Long helped stake out the town site of Uncompahgre and with the Cutler brothers built the third of three cabins that were to constitute the entire community that first winter. Long's cabin was selected by the La Plata County Commissioners to be the polling place for all of the sparsely settled Uncompahgre country. The La Plata Commissioners recognized the new community as Uncompahgre, but the post office designated it as Ouray. It was at Long's cabin that he cooked the famous Christmas dinner for the thirteen men wintering in Ouray. In celebrating the men drank from a gallon jug of vinegar. The hill where the cabin was located is still called Vinegar Hill. Long was petitioner for the 1875 application for the Town of Uncompahgre, was elected Trustee at the first town meeting of Ouray in 1876, and County Judge when Ouray County was formed.

Treatment of ore to free gold and silver was a real problem in the San Juans. The first ore from the Wheel of Fortune had to be packed on burros over the ridge of Imogene Basin, down to Silverton then over Cinnamon Pass to Lake City. To pay for that very long trip took very high ore values so ore was carefully sorted and the less valuable left on the dump. In 1877 it cost twenty-five dollars a ton to pack ore from Ouray to Silverton for treatment and then the result had to be carried by wagon to Pueblo for smelting. One mine was reported using 270 burros for that haul.

Long went back to Silverton, bought the equipment and works of the Brown, Epley & Company smelting plant and hauled it to Ouray. He bought other equipment from outside the San Juans and placed in operation the mill and smelter named San Juan & St. Louis Smelting Company, a name suggesting his ties to St. Louis. The plant was located just short of four miles north of Ouray.

Unfortunately for Ouray, enterprising Robert F. Long died in 1882 at age forty-one. He was a veteran of the Civil War, his wife a New Orleans' belle. Their eleven-year-old son died in St. Louis a month later. So it was not Robert Long who found the mine in Cow Creek which has been lost for so many years. It was Alfred E. Long who made the discovery. A. E. Long must have come into the San Juans before 1876 because he was well known enough to run for county clerk of the new San Juan County in that year. He lost in a three man race for the position. He was still involved in Silverton in 1879 when he was one of three men who incorporated a Silverton, Ophir and Rico Toll Road Company which never turned a spade of rock.

By this time A. E. Long's interest had been transferred to Ouray and he ran again for county clerk, but this time for newly formed Ouray County, and he was elected. He held public office on and off

The lost Cow Creek Mine would be in the rugged mountain to the left in the background of this old photograph of Ridgway. It is a very wild and rugged area
— COURTESY OF P. DAVID SMITH

for many years. In 1891 he founded the *San Juan Silverite*, a newspaper largely dedicated to his political aspirations. The short-lived paper was described as "a political paper with no party and a religious paper with no church."

Almost twenty years after his experiment of prospecting in the Animas country, Long decided to go gold hunting again. Most all the mountains deemed worthy of prospecting had been thoroughly covered and staked with mining cliams. But Long knew of one area that had been largely overlooked. He enlisted an acquaintance to go with him.

The two set out to prospect in Cow Creek country. Finding some promising float (rock that had rolled from higher up) led them to climb a high stony ridge leaving their horses below. There on the top of this bare ridge they found a six inch vein of quartz carrying good gold values. A heavy thunderstorm came up, and as there was no place on that barren ridge to seek shelter, the two men just continued to work at extracting gold-bearing quartz. A lightning bolt struck knocking Long's companion unconscious. When he recovered he found the bolt had killed Long. He packed Long's body across the back of a horse and led the animal with its burden back to Ouray.

Severely shocked, he told his story, climbed aboard the first train leaving Ouray and was never heard from again. He left behind the story of a rich gold mine and some ore to prove it, but no direction as to how to find it. The Cow Creek drainage is immense, but somewhere in that vastness, on a rocky ridge, is a rich lost gold mine.

CHAPTER 3 🌿

THE LOST MINE WITHIN SIGHT OF MAIN STREET

The cliffs rose so sharply and so high that the mountains seemed almost to lean over the valley below. "Yes," he thought. "This must surely be the place. But how the mountain valley has changed!" Forty-five years before the valley was covered with a thick evergreen forest; several small streams wandered freely across the valley floor and toward the river. Then it had been quiet and peaceful. Two days earlier he had been in the valley that now contained the town of Telluride, but without hot springs he knew it was not the place he was seeking, so he had taken the railroad and come to Ouray.

Now he stood in front of the three-story brick Beaumont Hotel, one of the finest hotels in all of Colorado. A contrast indeed to the worn tent he had slept in years ago. The boardwalks of the city stretched for four or so blocks in each direction. The trees were largely gone; a few great spruce and fir still pointed upward fifty to a hundred feet, and newly planted box elders were beginning to mark the edges of the streets.

Then the odors had been of the sweet evergreen trees and the smell of bubbling waters. Now hundreds of pack animals and teams left a far more pungent stink, particularly around the rail station and the lower part of town where the stables and corrals were located.

Hot springs still poured from three mountainsides, but buildings encased them to offer hot baths. Then it had been ever so quiet and still except for the winds that blew in the forest. Now, over the bark of dogs and the play of children, the staccato sound of the little narrow gauge steam locomotive could be heard as it switched in the rail yard.

But the mountains are the same and there are hot springs. "Yes, this is the place," he thought to himself, "this is the place — and right up there on that mountain must be the gold mine we found so many years ago."

He turned and went into the hotel entrance where the porter had been waiting impatiently with his luggage. He was a distinguished looking gentleman, well groomed with hair and beard showing more than a little grey. His clothing was that of an Easterner and his bags were of good leather. He looked the success that he was.

In the days that followed, he purchased rugged riding and hiking clothes and moved from the Beaumont Hotel into the smaller, friendlier frame building of the Western Hotel. There he was able to sit at the long tables when he took his meals amid the miners, salesmen and others who frequented the Western. He didn't talk much but listened carefully to the conversations that surrounded him and asked a few sharply angled questions. He was liked and respected by the other patrons.

Every morning after breakfast, he would disappear into the surrounding mountains, usually hiking, but occasionally riding, to be gone all day and to return worn and sore in the evening in time for supper. Afterwards he would take clean clothes, leave his dirty ones at the Chinese laundry just around the corner and go to the south edge of town to one of the bath houses that covered a steaming hot spring. There he would soak out the grime and soreness of the day.

Most of the summer went by in this manner; but finally as the cooler temperatures of August arrived, he took into his confidence one of his hotel companions who had lived many years in the Ouray region. Soon the two of them were making daily journeys together. The story that he told was an exciting one.

He was one of several men who were making their way back East from the California gold fields. They had decided to go far from the usual routes and traveled into what the Ute Indians called "The Shining Mountains." They had unexpectedly come upon the bowl where the City of Ouray now is located. Then it appeared that no white man had ever visited there, although they knew that mountain men must have trapped for beaver in the river. Mountain men had explored nearly every inch of streambeds that might be the home of beaver.

There were lots of signs of use by the Indians, who apparently camped frequently and long beside the hot springs — doubtlessly to soak away stiff joints and muscles. This was Ute Indian country they knew, and the Utes would make short work of intruders if they found them poaching upon ground which they considered sacred because of the healing hot springs.

The trip of the returning gold hunters had been an arduous one. They were tired and weary and had walked hundreds of miles since they had lost their horses crossing the great Utah deserts. So they settled down to rest and recuperate before resuming their eastward trek.

They had wandered into the bowl from the north where the Uncompahgre River flowed out into a broad arid valley. That seemed to be the only egress into the bowl since on the south great falls and cliffs made it impossible to escape, and to the east and west great sheer cliffs towered, broken only by waterfalls and cascading creeks. The bowl was almost completely surrounded except for the cut made by the Uncompahgre as it flowed outward to the north.

The days of rest in the lovely valley were life restoring. Game was plentiful and with the many wild plants, they had plenty to eat. But then came the day when their lookout spied a large party of Indians coming up the Uncompahgre to enter the valley. But where and how to go? The only ready exit was where the Indians were coming. To the south, it was impassable. Quickly they headed to one of the streams that fell down the mountain-sides in a series of plunges, and they began the exhausting climb upward.

As they climbed it was much like toiling up a great ladder. Their escape seemed to be successful, apparently the Indians had not seen them. Each day they were careful to destroy as much evidence of their occupation as was possible. And then it happened!

As one of the party grasped a ridge of stone to pull himself up, he suddenly realized it was a quartz ridge that contained gold. Now they were experienced California gold miners, and they recognized the richness of their find. What should they do? Below them the happy Indian children were playing. The women were making camp, and the men were already bathing in the hot waters. All seemed busy and completely unaware of the party of white men high above them.

The men decided to take a chance. They stopped their careful escape and began an attack on the ridge of quartz with their knives and a hatchet they carried. They pried out nuggets of almost pure gold. But such instruments could not be used a long time without the breaking and pounding of the hatchet being heard by the Indians below. The solution they followed was to build a hot, almost smoke-less, fire on the quartz ledge and let the heat of the fire "rot" out the

The lost mine within sight of Ouray's Main Street is located somewhere in this scene of the Oak Creek drainage. — AUTHOR'S PHOTO

chunks of rock holding the gold. This they did, and when night came, they carefully extinguished the fire in fear the Indians might see it. They spent a cold and nearly cheerless night.

The next morning the fire was rekindled, and the baking out of the gold resumed. But it was not long before the sharp eyes of a brave saw the smoke of the fire; the prospectors watched as he pointed the fire out to his companions. Soon the Indians started toward the cascading stream that led to the gold hunters.

It was time for the white men to go. Hastily they packed up the several hundred pounds of the almost pure gold they had mined and began a hurried climb up the ladder-like canyon. They were successful in eluding the Indians who after all had come to the Ouray valley to rest and play not to seek out enemies and go to war.

The party of prospectors eventually made their way out of the mountains, onto the plains and caught a wagon train going back East. The fortune they had mined on the cleft above Ouray made each of them prosperous.

Now one of them had returned to the lovely hidden valley in which they had rested some forty years before. But how it had changed. What he had earlier envisioned as an easy matter was now most difficult. He couldn't find the gold mine. Most of the land marks he had expected to guide him had been changed or removed. The streams running down to the river had been channeled into board flumes, and he could not tell where the original beds were. Now streets had been carved, great boulders removed and houses built. The forest in which they had once-upon-a-time camped was no longer there. The trees had been cut and milled for timber to build the new town. It was ever so confusing.

Day after day he looked for the mine that must be within sight of Ouray's Main Street, but he was unsuccessful. He finally paid an old-timer, who had lived through the great transformation of the valley from wilderness to a modern city, to help. But the two of them working together were still unsuccessful. He thought he had been certain of the mountainside his party had climbed to escape, but now he was uncertain. The two climbed all the cascading streams that dropped down into the town, but their search was unsuccessful.

Finally as autumn turned to winter, the distinguished gentleman repacked his bags, boarded an outgoing train and returned back East. He never came back, and no other seeker ever found the mine. So within sight of Main Street Ouray, Colorado, lies a lost gold mine. Someday someone will find great riches. Will it be you?

CHAPTER 4

HOW TO FIND A MINE — CONSULT A SEERESS

There are many strange stories about mines. Perhaps one of the strangest is of a mining operation on Cunningham Gulch outside of Silverton. The development of this mine was directed by a spiritual medium in far away New York City. According to the legend, the two Innis brothers, who lived in New York, inherited a considerable amount of money. They decided to multiply their fortune by finding a gold mine. How to find a gold mine? Their method was to consult a prophetess. She placed her finger on a map and told them if they dug where she pointed they would find a "lake of gold." Then she charged them $50,000 for the revelation.

Off the brothers went to find the "lake of gold." The place where the prophetess had placed her finger was at the head of Cunningham Gulch, which ran south from Howardsville. This small community was then the center of mining explorations in the San Juans. With utter confidence in the seeress' predictions, the brothers went to the San Juans, crossed rugged Stony Pass and descended to Cunningham Gulch and Howardsville. Then they set out to find the location of the mine that contained a "lake of gold." Back up Cunningham Gulch they went and started up the Cunningham Pass trail. A thousand feet above the gulch, at a point with a gorgeous view of the gulch all the way to Howardsville, they stopped. Here they decided was the place their seeress had told them they should mine. Here they would find the "lake of gold."

Rather than beginning mining immediately, they set out to provide for themselves as many of the comforts of home as could be obtained. While pack trains were bringing dining room furniture, bed sets and comfortable living room chairs, the brothers were building an elaborate house. Elaborate, that is, for that day and time in the rough San Juans. It became known as the "White House" with its painted lattice trim which gleamed for miles down the gulch.

That is the legend, and it is a good one, partially true and partially made of cobwebs. Actually the mine was originally discovered in 1871, very early in the history of the San Juans and the Animas River country. The stakers of the claim were John C. Dunn, David (Billy) Quinn, and Andrew (Andy) Richardson. The stories of these early pioneers are remarkable.

In 1869 Dunn teamed up with Adnah French to lead a party into the San Juans. The only known previous exploration had been done by the Baker parties in 1860-61. French had been in Baker's Park at that time. Dunn's earlier career as agent for the Apache-Navajo agency did the party good service, for they were able to negotiate Apache cooperation in crossing through Arizona and New Mexico to reach the Dolores River. But they arrived late in the season and were caught in an early and heavy snowfall. The expedition would surely have perished as they had neither the food or clothing to survive a San Juan winter, but French called upon his experience with the 1860-1861 Baker parties. The members of that expedition had built what they called Animas City down the Animas River quite a few miles from Baker's Park (the site of present day Silverton). After the Baker party retreated from the San Juans, Ute Indians had burned many of the cabins, but in 1869 perhaps thirty still remained, and they offered much needed shelter to the French-Dunn party until they could escape to New Mexico settlements. The following year of 1870 Dunn returned to prospect along the Dolores, and finally in 1871 he climbed over the towering mountains and high passes and reached the Animas River country.

Andy Richardson and Billy Quinn were making their first trip into the Animas country when they joined with Dunn in staking the Highland Mary. From this time forth they were integral parties in the development of the San Juans. In 1872 they were a part of the first Fourth of July celebration in the San Juans. It was held in Arrastra Gulch at the Little Giant. Old timers still tell about them repeatedly firing an overloaded musket until it exploded, its flying parts endangering those celebrating.

Along with others, Richarson and Quinn staked the Shenandoah that same year before retreating out of the territory for the winter. The Shenandoah was to become one of the greatest mines in the United States, and for several years only its production kept Silverton alive. But Quinn and Richardson had sold their interests years before the mine was fully developed. In 1873 Quinn and Richardson returned to participate in organizing the Copper Mountain Mining District, and somewhat later, the agricultural community of Hermosa, not too distant from old Animas City and much nearer the future Durango.

In 1874 an assay office opened in Howardsville, and Dunn, Richardson and Quinn went back to the Highland Mary, took some samples and had them assayed. The best assay ran $2,250 to a ton and caused considerable excitement. This resulted in Edward Innis becoming interested in the property. As the three owners did not have the necessary capital to develop a mine, they sold the Highland Mary to Innis in 1875, each receiving a reported $10,000. Free of their involvement in Animas properties, Quinn and Richardson sought new opportunities and hiked over the mountains and eventually discovered rich ore bodies in Imogene Basin, named by Richardson for the woman he was to marry. Their discoveries were to lead to the establishment of the Mt. Sneffels Mining District. It was Richardson who led Tom Walsh to what became the great Camp Bird Mine. Richardson owned the house in Ouray next to my boyhood home, and our home at one time was rented by Walsh to house his family while he developed the Camp Bird.

Edward Innis was one of two brothers with considerable holdings in New York and Pennsylvania. His brother George was an investment banker. There is no record of George coming to Silverton and the Highland Mary during the mine's early years. It was Edward who wanted action and sought the mining frontier. It appears he might have been involved in the initial financing of the Little Giant Mine; at least he was involved in the court cases seeking possession of the milling machinery, and he eventually ended up owning this famous property.

The Little Giant, which was discovered in 1872 was the first successful mine in all of the San Juans, and news of its success attracted the capital necessary to develop the San Juan mines and led to the founding of the towns of Silverton and Howardsville.

It does seem likely that Edward Innis did consult a medium and that she did indicate on a map where he would find a "lake of gold." That story is indelibly pressed into Silverton's legends. But where does legend stop and fact begin? We know that Innis had an interest in the Little Giant before he ever set foot in the San Juans. We also know during the winter before he came, that he tried to buy the High-land Mary but was unable to strike a deal with Dunn. It is highly unlikely that the map was of enough detail for the medium to specifi-cally designate the site of the Highland Mary. In fact we would have to question if a detailed map of the Animas country even existed in that year. More than likely the medium only indicated on some map the general vicinity of the San Juans. As the Animas country was where the only mining excitement was going on at the time, Innis would have come to Howardsville and Silverton. Was it possible that Innis (who seemed to have invested in the Little Giant) knew of the San Juans before he sought out the medium? Just when did he go to the medium—before or after—investing in the Little Giant?

If Innis had invested in the Little Giant (the court cases seem to prove that he did), isn't it likely that he would have consulted with some of those also involved and while in the San Juans learned of the Highland Mary? At any rate he unsuccessfully attempted to pur-chase the property before he ever came to Silverton. After arriving Innis carefully investigated several properties in the summer of 1875 before settling in the Highland Mary.

Innis began to develop the mine with confidence after his pur-chase in August, and by September thirty men were engaged in build-ing structures to house the mine operations. The one attracting the most attention was the "White House" located high in the mountainside looking down at the impressive valley of Cunningham Gulch. It was two stories and reportedly elaborately furnished for Innis' comfort. Innis started tunneling from the outcropping of the vein, but as it was composed mainly of silver he largely ignored it and went on his search for the "lake of gold." He did repeatedly consult his prophetess, and he often redirected drilling so that the resulting tunnel wandered all over the interior of the mountain.

By 1878 the Highland Mary had three levels with miles of tun-neling. That fall Innis had twenty tons of ore shipped directly to St. Louis where it was smelted and returned an amazing $1,900 to the ton! However Innis shipped so little ore that it could not cover the costs of digging the wandering mine, which he also attempted to keep open year round. In 1880 he imported a ton of hay during the winter. It had to be packed in on the backs of men on skis from the Rio Grande side of the Continental Divide via Cunningham Pass.

How many trips they made I have no idea, but the cost was immense. In that winter more than 100 avalanches were reported as thundering down the cliffs and slopes of Cunningham Gulch.

Eventually Edward Innis' control over the Highland Mary ended. With more traditional management and no help from a seeress, it became a smoothly operating property. The many silver veins that had been uncovered were profitably pursued. A mill to treat the ore was built below in the Cunningham Gulch valley and fed by tram. Production continued until it ended permanently in the late 1940s when a snowslide smashed and burned the mill and killed the watchman. Certainly the story of Edward Innis, his prophetess, and the Highland Mary continue to be told and retold.

This is the view down Cunningham Gulch from the Highland Mary Mine. It's a long way up!
— AUTHOR'S PHOTO

CHAPTER 5

OF OXEN AND BURROS AND MULES

According to old photographs oxen teams were heavily used in the transportation of supplies from railheads to Ouray, Telluride and Rico. I have never seen a photo of oxen teams in Silverton, but a few may have been used. By the time I came around, they were a thing of the past. The only time I ever saw an oxen team was when I was very, very young, and a farmer from Horsefly Mesa came into Ouray with a load of produce (probably potatoes). The occurrence was so unusual that a telephone call from my father at the grocery store summoned all of us kids to Main Street to view a scene from out of the past.

Dave Wood was the operator of the major freight line that came into the three San Juan communities, and old pictures show four spans of bulls pulling two great wagons. The mine owners and merchants complained about the high charges of Wood and looked forward to lower freight rates when the railroad arrived. To their surprise railroad freight charges were higher than Woods' hauling by oxen and mules. But speed of delivery was on the side of the railroad as was the fact that goods arrived in better condition.

Burros were always driven, for the contrary beasts could not be led without a tug-of-war ensuing. Two hundred pounds was a good load for a burro, although this was too often exceeded. Tradition says that one big advantage of the burro was that it could scavenge for itself and need never be fed hay or grain. In fact the great burro herds of Ashenfelter and Donald were kept so continuously on the trail that the animals had little time to forage on their own and were fed in the great burro corrals at the foot of Eighth and Ninth Avenues in Ouray down by the Uncompahgre River.

Of course the burro was the companion of the prospector and carried his tools, blankets and food in his lonely search for wealth. A number of yarns tell of the burro being the cause of the discovery of a rich lode when the prospector was retrieving his burro and stumbled upon an outcropping; or even one story that the burro led the prospector to a rich lode. Such is the story of Winfred Stratton, an itinerant prospector, who for years struggled in vain over the Colorado Rockies with a burro that grew thinner and more footsore as Stratton's clothing grew more ragged. Finally the two struck it rich in a rocky pasture that became Cripple Creek. Stratton had come early to the Colorado gold fields and spent his first two years in Colorado Springs where he became a successful carpenter and land investor. He gave this up in 1875 to invest in the Yretaba Silver Mine located in Cunningham Gulch, just outside Howardsville. It was a poor investment, but it led Stratton to further searches in the San Juans. With a partner named Adsit and two burros he went back to Cunningham Gulch. There Adsit located the North Star Mine, and soon was relaxing on the French Riviera. Stratton staked out the Silver Cross Lode which proved to be worthless. He returned to Colorado Springs for the winter, earned enough for a new grubstake, and then he was off again with his burro looking for the mine. Thus it went for years until he stumbled across his Cripple Creek find. Marshall Sprague said of Stratton, "He liked traveling around with a burro for a companion. Burros did not talk back, quibble, complain, belittle, overcharge, boast or make unreasonable demands. They just did what they were told."

Nicholas Creede had quartered for some years in Portland, four miles below Ouray, while he prospected. On one trip Creede and his burro headed over the Continental Divide and while trying to picket his burro he pounded against a rich quartz outcropping. "Holy Moses," he is reported as exclaiming, I've struck it rich!" So the famous Holy Moses Mine made the mining camp of Creede. The mine also made Nicholas Creede a very wealthy man who moved to California to live luxuriously, leaving his twenty-year burro companion behind, deserted and forgotten. The burro may well have ended his days pulling ore cars in the blackness of the Holy Moses.

Before Creede left for warmer California, he was a participant in locating two other mines, both found because of burros. Creede had sold the Holy Moses to David Moffat, then president of the Denver and Rio Grande Railroad. He did this because he was not financially able to develop the property, rich as it was. Reportedly Moffat paid Creede $75,000. The story of what followed was written by Richard Harding Davis the year following these events.

A prospector by the name of Renninger obtained a grub stake from a butcher at Wagon Wheel Gap, then a well known tourist camp to which the DR&G had run narrow gauge rails several years before in hopes of luring tourists seeking cures in the hot springs and to see the wonders of what was to become the Wheeler National Monument. While off prospecting, Renninger's three burros disappeared. Renninger followed many miles in "hot and profane pursuit" until he overtook them at Bachelor Mountain. Unsuccessful in getting the three to go back to camp, he sat down to await their pleasure. Sitting, he began a casual chipping on a nearby ridge which showed mineral in such quantities that he thought he had better seek more experienced advice and brought Creede to see it. Creede looked at it, and begged Renninger to define his claim at once. Renninger, offering up thanks to the three donkeys, did so and named it the Last Chance. Then Creede located next to his property, shoulder to shoulder, and named his claim the Amethyst. These became two of the fabulously rich mines of Creede fame. All from the contrariness of three burros!

Burros often became the pets of children and woman, and there are many excellent photographs that give evidence of this, sometimes including the burro in a family photograph. There is one Ouray picture of children playing teeter-totter using the back of a burro for the fulcrum.

In the gold rush of 1860, H. A. W. Tabor and his wife Augusta headed from Denver through South Park in an ox-pulled wagon attempting to reach Buckskin Joe. This was a new camp near present-day Leadville (non-existent then) but on the opposite side of the Mosquito Range from South Park. They found it almost impossible to cross the high mountains that blocked their route to the reported gold diggings beyond. Augusta wrote in her diary:

> The fourth day in the park we came late at night to Salt Creek. Tried the water and found we could not let the cattle drink it, neither could we drink it. We tied the oxen to the wagon and went supperless to bed. The night was very cold and a jack came to our tent and stood in the hot embers until he burned his fetlocks off.

The next day Tabor went off searching for the pass that would take them through the Mosquito Range. Augusta was left to guard the camp. It was a cold and miserable day; the baby fretted, the oxen were thirsty and restless. Night came and no Tabor. "I felt desolate indeed", wrote Augusta. Then the little burro who had come into camp the night before entered her tent. "I bowed my head upon him and wept in the loneliness of my soul."

The Rev. George M. Darley frequently used burros in his journeys through and over the San Juans. At one time he recalled:

"Burro punching" is a familiar term where the business is followed, and means to walk behind a pack train punching the patient, sure-footed and valuable, although greatly abused little animal. Often have I walked behind a burro when going to preach the Gospel in the "regions beyond." . . . . I regret that many believe the burro has cultivated the swearer as much as he has the state. Those who abuse the burro and swear at him like a pirate, curse everything; not because they are provoked, but because they are habitual swearers.

The general belief among packers seems to be that the burro has no feeling, knows no joy or pain and expects to be mistreated. Burros suffer terribly . . . . I admit they are hard to kill. A "baby burro" fell from the top of a cliff sixty feet in height, into the Gunnison River and was not injured. On Bear Creek Trail about five miles above Ouray, one packed with flour fell two hundred feet; the weight of the flour turned the burro heels up and striking in the snow, his life was saved. Yet the animal can be killed, and it sometimes dies a natural death. While crossing deep streams unless their ears are tied, they will drown; but by tying them up so they can be pulled across without danger . . . . As soon as his ears are untied his voice is loosened and he breaks forth in trumpet tones of rejoicing, loud enough to be heard far and near.

In winter of '79 a man brought a burro from Mineral Point, at the head of the Uncompahgre River, over Engineer Mountain, to the head of Henson Creek, on snow shoes. He made the shoes of sole leather and taught the burro to use them. It was slow work, yet he succeeded in getting his "Jack" across the range. . .

Burros were widely used in the mines of the San Juans to pull ore cars, loaded going in with supplies, and going out with rock.

Many burros may never again have seen daylight after they were brought into the mine's darkness. While the Revenue Mine was probably the first electrically powered mine in the world, still in the further recesses burros were used to pull cars of ore to the lifts which carried the ore to the main transportation tunnel where electric powered motors took over. When the Revenue changed over from mule and burro power to electric motors, it was found necessary to rebuild all ore cars. Until then axles were simply held in place by metal bushings; but with the increased speed, these bushings quickly burned out and it was necessary to replace them with bearings. When the Ranchers Mining Company reopened the Revenue Tunnel in the 1980s and pumped out the water that had flooded the lower workings for many years, they found at the lowest levels the stables of the burros that had once worked on that level, just as it was at the time of the fire which resulted in the abandonment of this level sixty years before.

A. E. Reynolds, who owned the Virginius-Revenue, was very cost conscious. He fed the 600 miners in his boarding houses with beef from his great ranch located near La Junta. The flour he used in baking also came from holdings in eastern Colorado where he ground flour from his immense wheat fields. As a rancher he appreciated good animals and the importance of keeping his investment in them protected; so he set up a rotation system assuring that his mules and burros were given "vacation time" to graze and recover strength before being returned to their underground duties.

John Ashenfelter followed Reynolds to the San Juan. Earlier he had been associated with Reynolds in hauling supplies to Reynolds' five Indian trading posts. When Ashenfelter arrived in Ouray he was so destitute he was forced to borrow money (probably from Reynolds) to buy a small herd of burros which were of sufficient number to haul supplies to the Virginius and return with ore to Ouray. As the mine developed and production increased, so did the pack trains owned by Ashenfelter.

By 1886 he was using from 200 to 300 jacks for packing and had seven six-mule teams on the road. During that year he delivered 1,500 tons of supplies and 100,000 feet of lumber (quantities of heavy lumber were needed to shore up mining tunnels, shafts and drifts) to the Virginius and other Sneffels mines. He carried out 2,965 tons of

A pack train is getting ready to leave the Cascade Grocery in the 1920's. The buildings are (left to right): The Cascade Grocery, Plaindealer office, Colombus Saloon, Ashenfelter's freight office, 220 Club and the Roma Saloon. — AUTHOR'S FAMILY COLLECTION

ore to Ouray. By the time of the Silver Panic of 1892 Ashenfleter had 100 wagons as well as 300 pack animals in use. By that time the mule teams had largely been supplanted by heavy draft horses. When his long trains of wagon headed out from Ouray to Sneffels, the train was headed by Ashenfelter's full-time veterinarian who rode back and forth along the train watching drivers and horses. Ashenfelter took good care of his valuable horses, mules and burros, for they were source of his success and wealth. Woe to the teamster or puncher who mistreated his stock. Even in 1897 (after the great Silver Crash) the *Ouray Herald* reported "Ashenfelter alone has 265 pack animals on the trail, besides a large number of sixes and several four-horse teams."

Mules had the advantage of being stronger than burros and could carry loads of from 300 to 400 pounds, depending upon terrain, and whether the going was up or down. Mules were led in long strings in contrast to the burros which were herded. The halter of each mule was tied to the pack saddle or tail of the mule in front. Good mules represented a major investment and reputable stables took care of their animals, making sure shoes were properly fitted and in the winter topped with cork. Both John Donald and John Ashenfelter had ranches where injured or tired stock could be rested and cared for.

Mules were both intelligent and full of idiosyncrasies. A packer soon learned to recognize each animal, call them by name, and treat each with respect. The mule inherited the better qualities from both sides of his parents. From the burro came his sure-footedness and his patience, from the horse came vigor and spirit, and from some unknown place came intelligence and steadiness.

A string of mules usually numbered fifteen to eighteen with a packer leading the train. Mules soon learned to be trailwise, carefully hug into the side of the mountain and not to step onto snow on the cliff side, which horses were apt to do. If a mule did sink down off the trail he stayed quiet until his packer could pull him to safety; a horse in the same situation usually would fight in panic, bedding itself deeper and deeper until it was impossible to rescue and had to be shot.

Trails to the mines were narrow and steep, with bends around large rocks which jutted out into the trail. Navigating such bends required care by both the packer and the mules. The packer would slow up, and each mule in turn would edge around the corner being careful not to pull either the mule ahead or behind off balance.

Sometimes it was impossible to break down heavy machinery into what was usually a small enough weight to be carried by a single mule. Such a 700 pound load had to be hauled from Telluride to the Tom Boy Mine, about six miles of tough trail. The packers selected a strong, smart mule and then fashioned a sort of sawhorse over the back of the mule and loaded the 700 pounds of machinery on top of that. The legs of the sawhorse were not long enough to dig into the ground while the mule advanced, but when the load became unbearable the mule could squat down, letting the load be supported by the legs of the sawhorse. In only a few moments the mule learned the trick and carried the 700 pounds the six miles with appropriate rest as the animal decided necessary.

Normally the load would have been either carried on a sling between two mules in tandem or "skidded". Heavy machinery was placed on skids and dragged up the mountain trails. That is how much of the heavy machinery that we see now at abandoned mines was delivered. One of the more horrible stories of mistreatment that I have heard was told to me by Tom Fellin, a schoolmate of mine and a respected and successful Ouray business man. The story was of the skidding of extremely heavy machinery to the Sutton Mine on the top of Mt. Hayden and overlooking the Uncompahgre Gorge at Bear Creek Falls. The remains of the old Sutton tram can still be seen on the side of Mt. Hayden opposite the Bear Creek Falls, and the old Sutton Mill stood just to the south of the falls until sometime in the '70s when a hiker, caught in a rainstorm, sought shelter in the old building, built a fire on the wooden floor and burned the historical old mill down. Some seventy or eighty horses, mules and burros were rounded up, harnessed and placed in a long string single file. When the trail became so steep that the animals could drag the heavy equipment no further, they were backed in their traces and at a given signal men and boys stationed at intervals along side the string would shout and whip the poor animals so that they would lunge into their collars. The sudden effort would move the load up the trail perhaps fifty feet when it would come again to a stop. Then the process was repeated over and over. Plunging into their collars (which were probably ill fitting) often resulted in broken collar bones. The injured animals were supposedly unhitched and shoved over the cliff. This I might note, was late in the history of the San Juans and after the deaths of both Ashenfelter and Donald.

Thomas Griffith, in his "San Juan Country," tells of a problem the Tom Boy Mine, high above Telluride, faced in getting its daily production of bullion from the mine to the train in Telluride. The situation in Telluride might be described as "unsettled." A vicious strike of miners against mine management had left hard feelings and the possibility of disgruntled miners holding up a shipment seemed probable. Then too the Camp Bird Mine recently had a shipment taken from the stage, to which it had entrusted its bullion, by armed bandits. So how to get the bullion, produced in a daily basis, from the mine to the railhead in Telluride was a problem. The solution came by selecting a particularly trustworthy mule and each day attaching the mule to the end of the pack string that moved from Telluride to the mine. Once at the mine the mule was unfastened and led unobserved to the retort room. There two bricks of bullion, one for each pannier (the bags that hung on either side of the pack saddle), were loaded. While heavy the bricks did not leave a noticeable bump to the casual observer. The mule's lead was then wrapped around the pack saddle and she was turned loose and became one of the nameless number of horses and mules that had been ridden or led to the mine and then turned loose to return to the stable. Although the mule might pause to nibble on a tuft of grass, she would not let a miner seeking a free ride catch her. And so she arrived discreetly at her barn to be unloaded and the bullion put on the waiting train. If, as Griffith says, the mule was late in arriving, the train was held until she did make it.

The care the packer had for his mules is also told by Griffith. Two trains of mules had battled their way through a storm for thirty six hours to reach snowbound Ironton with needed supplies. Both mules and packers were near collapse when they arrived and unloaded their packs. Then they discovered there was no stable room. With exhausted animals, a blizzard blowing and no shelter, many of the mules would die before the next morning. After a search the packers found an unoccupied two story building — a brothel which had been boarded up while the proprietress went to warmer climes. Over violent protests, the packers forced the door open and deployed the animals upstairs and downstairs, in rooms and hallways. Deluxe carpets were slashed by sharp hooves, and hay and oats were fed from bureau drawers. It was said some of the animals bedded down on beds used for other activities. Later the owner of the pack trains gladly repaid the damages. Each of his mules was worth "far more than the price of a fancy lady's cubicle."

A writer in "Hoof Prints" from the *Grand Junction Sentinel* wrote that "miners and skinners have noted each mule had a personality that differs from any other mule. The mule is thought to have a better memory than an elephant and will never forget a person who treats him badly. The mule will take advantage of the opportunity to get even if that person should step behind him. A mule will not overeat or drink too much like a horse will. He exhibits self control."

The mules that worked underground became personalities and often pets to many of the miners. Not only were the mules pets, they were companions. The miners lavished their affection on the mules. David Lavender, in his wonderful book **One Man's West**, tells of spending one year at the Camp Bird Mine during the Great Depression years. Three mules were working with the miners. One was a real "sweetheart" that sought attention from the miners, nudging them for petting and treats. Miners in the area of the mine where old Buck was worked saved an apple core or a tidbit from their lunch pails to feed him. Then there was the brisk and business-like Jen. This mare

Freight ore wagons hauling ore to the Tomboy Mine about 1910 or 1912. Marion Sams is in the first wagon and Burt Lansberry in the second. — COURTESY OF P. DAVID SMITH

ignored everyone but her driver and fell straight to her duties with efficiency. She knew she should pull four cars, and if another was attached she would stand still looking over her shoulder until the offending fifth car was removed and then would immediately go about her responsibilities. Her detached attitude did not result in the miners giving special attention to her. Lavender said she reminded him of the trim, neat business-like women.

The third mule was Cooney, a "Peck's bad boy." Sometimes he would run away with a string of cars. A "brandishing stick" sent him into a fury. He would reach out and bite an offending miner. One summer the superintendent who attempted to herd him in the pasture threw a chunk of wood at him. The result was a chase of the super all over the hill until finally the man was treed up a power pole where Cooney kept him for half an hour. One fall Cooney was led up the steep rock trail to Level Two, high above Level Three where most of the work was going on. Cooney took advantage of the steep trail, catching his driver off balance and running away. Because of the battle involved in leading him from Level Two to the barn and back, he was ultimately penned inside the mouth of the tunnel where he could look out, see sunlight and bray at the other two. But then an early storm filled up the tunnel portal, and the trail back to the barn was blocked. It was dark and lonesome inside that tunnel. His tantrums did no good and neither did his braying. He was there for "half a year of meditation." A tiny lift connected Two and Three Levels, and each day hay and grain were sent up by the lift, and a miner would climb the 300 foot ladder to feed Cooney. When his feeder arrived, Cooney would cry with a "pathetic joy" and seek any kind of attention. If there was some work for him to do (not often or very long) he was delighted, and when the chore was done he visibly drooped. When the miner climbed back down the ladder he left a carbide lamp burning to offer some poor light for a few hours. The bray of the mule as the miner departed was heartbreaking.

Finally spring arrived and the tunnel entrance became free. After a wait to let his eyes adjust to sunlight, the crew released Cooney. He ran like a small boy up and down the mountain meadow, kicking, rolling on the ground and then running and jumping again. All expected him to return to his old ways, but he became a model pet looking for pats and tidbits with never a nip or a bite at a miner. He would, however, still show his distaste and intent if threatened with an uplifted stick, but Cooney's long winter in darkness and solitude had changed his personality.

Hanging around the stables and listening to the punchers and skinners while a small boy was an educational experience for me. We heard many stories of the mines and the men who found them. And we learned stories about the most prominent citizens of Ouray and the San Juans that have never been printed and perhaps never should be. We learned the origin of the unusual name given to one of the mules — it was the same as one of the girls on Second Street, who had knifed her boyfriend in a most peculiar manner; and the way and aim of that mule certainly earned her that name.

It would be improper to close this reminiscence without a comment on the "song" of the burro and to his somewhat less endowed mule relative. The burro was often called the "Rocky Mountain Canary," and one fun loving Colorado legislator proposed the State Bird, the Lark Bunting, be replaced with the Rocky Mountain Canary. The proposal was passing until the speaker rapped the bill out of order.

The *Denver Tribune* of June 1, 1871 reported that in Clear Creek Mining District a preacher was exhorting his congregation, quoting from the Bible, "Hark, I hear an angel sing!" Just at that moment a burro grazing nearby broke loose with his peculiar song. Wisely the minister made no effort to restore calm in his laughing audience.

In 1889 Rev. George M. Darley, the pioneer minister of the San Juans who with a burro made an epic journey through snow and bitter cold some 120 miles from Lake City to Ouray, wrote that one Sabbath evening his son's burro was hitched to a post near the back of the church. "Sure enough", wrote Darley, "when I was well into my sermon Maude began. First a solo - low, clear, penetrating, not altogether unmusical, then a kind of duet, the outgoing breath making one kind of noise, the incoming another. This was followed by a quartet composed of the most hideous noises that it was possible for any of her species to make. By that time I had stopped; but Maude, true to her nature, continued. The congregation could not contain themselves, for the burros of the neighborhood began answering, and I really think from the way that Maude then let out her voice that she thought it was an encore."

Living with burros, as we did years ago in the San Juans, we became used to their braying to some degree. I remember one burro in Ouray that always brayed at exactly the same time each morning and was so regular her bray could be used as an alarm clock. When on a very seldom occasion, she brayed at a different time, it threw all the neighborhood off of their morning schedule. Somehow teachers were unwilling to accept the true reason for tardiness when we explained, "We're late because the Hopkin's burro didn't bray on time."

When Cy Warman wrote his immortal poem on Creede, he did not forget the burro:

Here's a land where all are equal-
Of high or lowly birth-
A land where men make millions,
Dug from the dreary earth.
Here the meek and mild-eyed burros
On mineral mountains feed.
It's day all day in daytime.
And there is no night in Creede.

CHAPTER 6 🌿

SNOW SNAKES AND SNOW MOSQUITOES

Cross-country skiing is gaining increased popularity. And well it should. It is a way to see and enjoy the spectacular San Juan Mountains in their winter beauty without the crowds of tourists who invade when summer comes. Whole families are enjoying the backcountry on skis and it seems to be a most wholesome way of having fun. But I do tremble when I see the very small children struggling with skis. Let me forewarn parents. This could be a winter of snow snakes.

As any hardy old-time prospector knows who has spent a winter snowed-in in some remote mountain cabin, when the snow is deep, the snow snakes breed. Please be careful and watch over your little ones when out in the backcountry in the winter.

Perhaps if I relate the story of old "Swede" Swanson, you will better understand about what I am warning you. The "Swede," as he was called by those who frequented Ouray's Second Street, spent his lonely winters in a small log cabin, high up in Grey Copper Gulch. The trail to the Swede's cabin led through several snowslide areas making it very unsafe to travel in the winter. In fact, the first death from a snowslide in the Ouray part of the San Juans was in Grey Copper Gulch. The trail was unsafe even for the Swede who was an expert in using the long twelve foot Norwegian snowshoes (skis to you). The winter of 1892 began unusually early, and the snow fell often and deep. By Thanksgiving Day the Swede was in isolation.

This particular winter turned out to be different from the usual lonely ones of the Swede's experience. With the first snowfall the Swede found a cute little snow snake. It was so cute, as it crawled from one snow bank to the next, that the Swede decided to make a pet of Herman, as he called the snow snake.

The old Swede took Herman into his cabin, but as anyone who knows ANYTHING about snow snakes knows, a snow snake needs ice and snow and is most comfortable when the temperature is below zero; twenty below is just fine. So if the old Swede was to keep Herman well and happy, Herman had to be out in the cold. The

Swede emptied a Hercules 4XXX wooden box of giant powder, and in it made a nest directly outside the front door for Herman. When Herman was tiny, that worked very well.

Snow snakes live largely on snow mosquitoes. Eating snow mosquitoes works out pretty well for snow snakes. You see, in the fall when snow snakes first hatch out, snow mosquitoes are also very tiny. Tiny enough for tiny snow snakes to easily dine upon them. Then if the balance of nature is most fortunate, snow mosquitoes grow to quite a large size. Snow snakes grow as rapidly as snow mosquitoes which is very fortunate, because as they dine on snow mosquitoes the snakes keep the mosquito swarms down in size. If the mosquito swarms got too big they would have to look elsewhere than the high mountains for food. Then they might descend into our mountain valleys and carry away our cats, small dogs, lambs and even small children. One of the real reasons that elk come into the valleys in the winter is to escape from snow mosquitoes.

But back to Herman. As he got bigger the Swede found the dynamite box could not keep him penned in. So the old Swede fitted a collar for Herman and tied him outside his cabin door. But tied up Herman was unable to catch enough mosquitoes to keep alive. The old Swede was forced to share his bacon with Herman. By Christmas it was apparent to the Swede that at the rate Herman was growing (and his appetite equally increasing) that if both he and Herman continued to eat bacon, the whole winter supply would soon run out.

So the Swede stopped eating bacon and went on a vegetarian diet. Now going on a vegetarian diet in the winter in the high mountains is a bit difficult. This meant having to dig down ten or twelve feet through snow to find dandelion greens or parsnip roots. To find enough food for himself the Swede had to give up working his claim so he could have more time to dig for foodstuffs.

Well Herman just kept growing on his diet of bacon. Luckily by the middle of January the snow mosquitoes had grown to be as big as Blue Jays, and the Swede could shoot them with his shot gun. Not only did this provide Herman with adequate food, it also solved the Swede's food problem. The Swede found that snow mosquitoes, when skinned and fried, made a tasty dish. He also discovered that the skins could be tanned and used to make bigger collars for the ever-growing Herman.

By February the snow mosquitoes were as big as geese, and

This W.H. Jackson photograph shows how the snow can accumulate in the Colorado mountains. The snow snakes and snow mosquitoes love this kind of weather!
— COURTESY OF P. DAVID SMITH

Herman was now as long as a South American Python. The Swede was spending most of his time out with his shot gun hunting for snow mosquitoes to feed Herman. No wonder that Herman was the biggest and fattest of all bull snow snakes!

One day in March while the Swede was out hunting, Herman suddenly discovered he was of age, and he sent out his mournful mating call. Have you ever heard a snow snake wail? Well it's just about the saddest sound that ever was; it sends shivers down your back. Herman wailed long and loud; his voice was so strong and healthy that it carried not only over the gulch, but up and down mountainsides. Soon all the lady snow snakes on Red and Brown Mountains were on their way to find out just what bull snow snake this could be that had such a powerful and attractive mating call.

The snow snakes came to the cabin, first one-by-one, then by twos and finally by the dozen. And big healthy and fat Herman made them all welcome. It was after their nuptial activities that the old Swede arrived back at the cabin with five snow mosquitoes hung over his shoulder. (Five was all he could carry on Norwegian snow-shoes going through deep drifts.) That throng of snakes was so hungry after their activity that five snow mosquitoes weren't anywhere near enough. After snapping the snow mosquitoes up, they enjoyed the next best thing, the Old Swede.

So parents as you enjoy family outings in the back country, keep a close watch over the little ones. Who knows? Herman might still be alive!

CHAPTER 7

IS BIGNESS, SMARTNESS?

Bigness isn't necessarily smartness. It's really amazing the number of stupid decisions big mining companies have made in the San Juans. Well perhaps they have followed the same stupid errors smaller mining men have made.

There was the crew working late one fall in Imogene Basin who had a contract to extend the tunnel of the Gertrude Mine. The snowslides started running, and at that high altitude and because of the unprotected location of the Gertrude, the crew became understandably nervous. In their anxiety to complete their contract and get out of the precarious situation they were in, they failed to examine or sample the last ten feet of the tunnel they were digging. At the blast that marked the completion of their contract, the crew slapped their belongings on their jackasses and hurriedly skittered downhill to warmth and safety. The ten feet of diggings they had failed to sample contained the fabulous gold ore that was to become the storied Camp Bird Mine.

But what about the superintendent of the company owning the Gertrude? William Weston had taken assaying at the Royal School of Mines in his native England, traveled to Del Norte, crossed Stony Pass to Silverton and by August of 1877 had crossed over into Imogene Basin and staked a number of claims including the Gertrude. By September, 1878 he deeded the Gertrude to two of the area's top mining engineers, H. W. and Caleb Reed, in return for which the Reeds were to run a tunnel of fifty feet to cut both the Gertrude and the Una. This is the tunnel the workers failed to sample, and both the Reeds and Weston failed to follow-up to see what the tunnel might have uncovered.

Weston then sold the properties to Allied Mines, a newly organized corporation with big, big plans of mining in Imogene Basin. Weston was named manager. Like too many young mining ventures, much of their capital was spent upon buildings and milling equipment before mines were even producing, and Allied went broke, owing money to many of the merchants in Ouray. So those properties owned by Allied lay dormant. Then Andy Richardson, working for Tom Walsh, saw the gold values on the Gertrude dump and the great Camp Bird Mine began. Well educated mining engineers, Caleb, H. W. Reed, and William Weston all failed to check and see what results had come from the extension of the tunnel they had paid for! With these examples of men who should have known better, perhaps we should not be too hard on the really big companies for their similar errors. But it is difficult.

Let us look at the Sunnyside Mine. In 1896 John Terry, the principal owner, who was in severe financial trouble, hit a rich pocket of gold and was able to sell the mine to New York interests for about $100,000 down and the remainder of the $200,000 purchase price to be paid within a year. As superintendent they hired the famous mining engineer T. A. Rickard. Rickard became an absentee superintendent, preferring the comfort of Denver life to the cold and wet of Eureka and hired a young inexperienced man to manage the on-site operation. Grandiose plans for a big new mill and new trams to carry ore from the mine were made and site preparation done. Then the rich pocket of ore pinched out and the New Yorkers let the mine go back to Terry without making the remaining payments due. The rest is history. Terry took the $100,000 and for the first time had the capital to properly develop the mine. The Sunnyside became a great producer.

Terry died in 1910. In that year, despite a depression in mining, the Sunnyside employed 108 men and had ten miles of underground workings. In 1917 the mine was bought by United States Smelting and Refining Co. The famed and huge Gold Prince Mill at Animas Forks was demolished and its machinery and steel used to erect an even bigger mill at Eureka for the Sunnyside. It was no longer just a gold mine but also produced zinc and lead.

By the end of 1920, plunging mineral prices closed the Sunnyside with almost 500 men laid off. Within a year it was operating again and became the first mine in Colorado to mill 1,000 tons a day. The crash of 1929 resulted in another closing, but it was reopened for a couple of years in the late 1930s.

The United States Smelting and Refining Co. brought a hot-shot expert to Silverton to evaluate the future of the Sunnyside. He arrived from Durango on the evening run of the D& R G Railroad, spent the night at the Grand Imperial Hotel, and had breakfast the next morning. He then stepped out of the hotel to Blair Street, slipped and landed on his rear. Angered and in pain, he never went to Eureka to see the mine or the mill, but climbed onto the next train going back to Durango and New York. His recommendation was to abandon and scrap the Sunnyside. The great mill was torn down; Eureka abandoned. Mark up one big boo boo.

In 1958 a uranium mining company secured a lease on the Sunnyside and took a radically different approach. Instead of mining from the high altitude of Lake Emma, the company went to the much lower and easily accessible American Tunnel of the Gold King at Gladstone. A mile extension of the American Tunnel put miners 600 feet below the deepest workings of the Sunnyside. Its lead-zinc ore was most profitable, but a vein of rich gold which was encountered drove away the original intent of mining lead and zinc. A high priced "expert" determined this was only another pocket and recommended mining the known reserves and then closing the mine. The reserves were mined, and the company overwhelmed with losses from a failed copper mining effort in Arizona, went into bankruptcy in 1971, closing down the Sunnyside while owing its miners weeks of salary. Another superintendent turned the mine around, and soon discoveries of new veins made the Sunnyside the biggest gold producer in Colorado if not the biggest on the continental United States. Again the owners made unprofitable investments in areas other than mining and went into bankruptcy.

This time the mine was sold to a new company which again made the Sunnyside into a major producer. However the scheme that revitalized the Sunnyside left operations carrying far too much overhead for its capitalization. To meet this expense required the mine and mill to work at great production levels. The experts once again said the Sunnyside was not viable. Miners were laid off, the American Tunnel was closed with a great cement plug, and today the Sunnyside lies a dead mine. Without the requirements of satisfying an over inflated capitalization and a mill that required such great amounts of ore to operate efficiently, could the Sunnyside be made into an operating mine again?

The great mining companies seem to be driven by the concept of "big is good". It is not worth their time and attention to work at any mining that is not gigantic. And so we come to the story of the

Revenue-Virginius. This legendary mine was one of the great silver producers. The winter of 1877 was the first the Virginius was worked. The four owners lived in a cabin that was so covered with snow they had to dig themselves out every morning. Then came the half-mile walk to the mine and digging their way to the portal. In spite of these hardships they succeeded in developing a good prospect and happily sold out the next summer. It was marketed again before reaching the hands of A. E. Reynolds who made the Virginius into one of the nation's great producers.

Because the snow and cold at an altitude of 12,300 feet was so dangerous in the winter and because it was impossible to build a road that wagons could use to carry out ore and bring in supplies, a lower tunnel was eventually driven at Sneffels at 10,750 feet. The Revenue Tunnel, 7,400 feet in length, also eliminated the high cost of pumping water up 1,700 feet, got rid of the expensive use of pack trains and made possible a great mill to process low grade ores which had been unprofitable at the higher Virginius. As the years went by, the mine suffered a fire, the mill burned, and the Revenue-Virginius closed.

In the 1980s a small mineral firm, the Ranchers, secured the Revenue and began a critical examination. Robert Larson, the superintendent, uncovered the old Virginius vein, and it was determined by Ranchers that with careful development it would again become a producer, although never as great as it had been at one time. Ranchers was bought out by one of the big mining companies which quickly brought the development to a close. It simply wasn't big enough for them to be bothered with. At least a million dollars in ore still sits in the mine ready to be shipped.

The inside of this mill under construction demonstrates just how big some of these building were. Some mines had as many as 500 men on the payroll. .— COURTESY OF P. DAVID SMITH

CHAPTER 8 🌵

THE SCRATCHED ASS MINE

A quartet of prospectors camped on a mining claim of only limited potential, found themselves shy in their larder and decided to go hunting for a deer. Their claim was one of the three Red Mountains which are located about half-way between Silverton and Ouray. The four were like many of the hunters of today. In order to prepare themselves adequately for hunting, they liberally indulged themselves from the several bottles they had stored in their tent.

Off they hiked, with an occasional stagger, sometimes remembering to gaze about for a deer, which after all, was the intent of their hike. One of the party, a Scot named Andy Meldrum, while tippling a bottle to his lips, misstepped while placing his foot on a loose rock and went tumbling to the ground. Andy landed on his seat on the errant rock's sharp edges. The sharp rock cut through his pants and into the flesh of his rear. Rising with an oath he kicked the errant stone downhill until it rolled with force against a protruding rocky ledge and splintered revealing a bright metal. After examining the rock the four determined it was mineral-bearing ore. As the rock had originally been on the top of a ridge, it was impossible for it to have rolled from a higher point, and the four immediately set out to stake a claim which was officially named the Yankee Girl.

The mine, while officially named "Yankee Girl", was not called by that name by the miners, teamsters and punchers in Ouray. As a boy I spent what might be regarded as too much time around the stables of Johnnie Donald and learned from the crew who labored in those corrals and barns that the mine's common name was the "Scratched Ass Mine."

The name "Scratched Ass Mine" isn't found in any of the history books about the Red Mountains that I have ever read. Obviously it was too earthy and like entirely too much of the history of yesterday in this country, this wonderful colorful bit of historical humor has long been forgotten. Forgotten also is the story that the mine was found by four hard drinking and drunk prospectors. In fact no consistent story seems to exist as to how and who made the discovery.

Author P. David Smith in his "Mountains of Silver" (the most complete telling of the story of the Red Mountains) credits the finding to "experienced prospector" John Robinson who on August 14, 1882 was out hunting when he sat down to rest and while seated spied a nearby rock which he instantly recognized as rich galena ore. Robinson identified the exposed ledge of ore from which the rock came and staked out a claim for himself and his three partners Andrew Meldrum, A. E. Lang, and August Dietlaf.

Well perhaps it was Robinson and not Meldrum who found the Yankee Girl, but I'll bet any amount of money that his "sitting" came from stumbling, and that he had a bleeding rear end. There are any number of versions of this story. Some say that it was only Lang (always called "Gus" and never by his initials of A. E.) and "Gus" Dietlaf (never known as August) who were with Robinson, and that Meldrum had grubstaked the other three and was at the time a blacksmith working above Telluride at the Sheridan Mine. Personally I favor the story told to me three-quarters of a century ago by the men who lived and worked around the mines of the Red Mountains.

The four men who found the Yankee Girl Mine a year earlier had located the Guston Mine. At this early time it didn't seem as though the silver in the ore of the Guston was rich enough to warrant development. It was very rich in lead, and as lead was needed badly as a flux at the local smelters to extract silver, it was worked to a limited extent for that purpose. The lead was packed all the way over the top of Red Mountain Pass and down to Silverton which had an operating smelter. For many years Silverton was the natural access to the mines of Red Mountain because of the difficulty in reaching Ouray through the Uncompahgre Canyon.

Clearly the Guston was discovered almost exactly a year earlier than the Yankee Girl, and it was producing, although not particularly rich ore. Thus it seems likely that Meldrum was probably a blacksmith at the Sheridan in the year of discovery, 1881; but it also seems probable that in 1882, when the Yankee Girl was staked, that he had left the Sheridan to work the producing Guston.

The finders had no idea that the ore of both the Yankee Girl and the Guston was in "chimneys" rather than in veins as was the usual

This photograph taken by the author shows the last remaining store in Red Mountain Town crumbling into ruins. Now it is hard to find even a piece of lumber in the area.
— AUTHOR'S PHOTO

case. Traditional mines were often "open cut" in early working to obtain the ore. As the development proceeded, tunneling was used. In both the Yankee Girl and Guston the chimneys could only be mined in shafts. Shaft mining was expensive. According to the Colorado Mining Directory of 1883, the Guston had one tunnel of sixty feet, but the Yankee Girl had two shafts of 70, 80 and 100 feet and a 100 foot tunnel cutting the bottom of the two shafts. After claiming the Yankee Girl the four men also staked the nearby Robinson and Orphan Boy. In 1883 the Robinson was reported as having a forty-foot tunnel.

Meanwhile the four discoverers had sunk a discovery shaft of twenty feet and shipped 4500 pounds of ore to Ouray by burro train. The ore ran eighty-eight ounces of silver per ton and was fifty-six percent lead. They sold the mine for $125,000 to eastern interests, as they lacked the capital necessary to develop the mine which later became one of the nation's richest and most storied silver mines. Smith in his comprehensive history of the Red Mountains lists the purchasers as O. P. Posey, George Crawford of Pittsburgh, L.J. Atwood of Waterbury, Connecticut and James Irvine of Lima, Ohio. Posey had been associated with the San Juans since 1874 when he became part owner of a hardware store in partnership with Alva Adams in Del Norte, where they served as bankers for both Del Norte and Silverton until a bank was established.

In 1878 Posey had bought the North Star Mine in Silverton. With Adams Posey opened a hardware store in Silverton, and in 1879 after splitting with Adams, he built Silverton's most impressive building to date. It was of brick with massive iron columns and stands today as the Lemon Tree building. While the others involved in buying the Yankee Girl were newcomers, they could depend on experienced and wealthy Posey for guidance. Interestingly the 1883 Mining Directory does not list Posey as an officer in the Yankee Girl Mining Company but gives James McKay of Pittsburgh as President, L.J Atwood as vice president, W.J. Hammond as secretary and treasurer and George Crawford as general manager. It also says the company now owned the Orphan Boy which had a forty-foot shaft with ore assaying at forty percent lead and fifty ounces of silver per ton. As the shafts went deeper in the two claims, the ore got richer and richer. Sixty men were employed with some values of 174 ounces of silver per ton. Various estimates are that the Yankee Girl produced from seven to ten million dollars. How unfortunate it was that the original four discoverers had to sell the mine for $125,000 because of lack of capital for development!

CHAPTER 9

ANDY MEETS A DIFFERENT KIND OF GOLD DIGGER

The history of prospectors who "hit it rich" seems to be that they either reinvested their money on some hole in the ground that never paid off, or they blew it in riotous living. In either instance they lost the money. The story of Andy Meldrum adds the dimension of losing the money to a gold digger.

Meldrum received $32,500 from the sale of the Yankee Girl. Most of us would agree with his decision to invest that money in a safer way to make a living than in mining. After spending cold winters at high altitude mines he went to much warmer Delta where he bought a ranch. It was the site of the old beet sugar factory which was just recently torn down. He bought some pure-blooded horses and stocked the ranch with Galloway cattle which came from his Scotch highland ancestry.

Across the river was a ranch occupied by Joe Bond and his daughter Polly. The two had recently come from Leadville where Bond operated a saloon. Polly had met a man named Charlie Mitchell in Leadville and was infatuated with him. Mitchell's reputation was anything but that of a good character. He did some prize fighting but had a nefarious reputation. Andy fell hard for Polly and soon was seeking her hand in marriage. At that time Polly was nineteen while Meldrum was in his thirties.

Bond urged Polly to look with favor on the attentions of wealthy Andy Meldrum. John Robinson (Meldrum's partner in the Yankee Girl) even overheard Polly's mother telling her to be careful how she talked to Andy and behave nicely to him so she could get her hands on his cash.

The two married on December 3, 1884. At that time Meldrum's wealth might have totaled about $50,000 plus an interest in the Guston mine which was beginning to pay real dividends to its stockholders. During their fifteen months of marriage Andy deeded the ranch at

Delta to Polly, and because she wanted to live in a more sophisticated community than Delta, he built her a $12,500 house in Denver,
a huge sum in relation to the value of the dollar in 1884. In addition
he bestowed $2,000 in cash upon her.

Toward the last of their fifteen months of marriage, Polly told Andy
she was not in good health, and she needed a trip to California.
Coincidentally her love interest, Mitchell, was touring California in
his role as prize fighter. (He had fought John L. Sullivan two times
without being knocked out.) Polly wasn't gone long before Andy
received notice she was seeking a divorce which Andy did not contest. The property in Delta was awarded to Polly, but only the property she received shortly before beginning divorce proceedings was
conveyed back to Andy.

Meldrum appealed to the Colorado Supreme Court seeking return
of all the real property conveyed to Polly during the entire marriage.
The grounds were undue influence, misrepresentation, and deceit on
the part of Mary, as Polly now called herself. Mary (Polly) was
represented by two lawyers, Patterson and Thomas, both of whom
had been United States senators and one was to be a Colorado governor. The testimony was overwhelming that Polly married Andy with
the intention of taking him for all of his wealth. Andy did regain the
Denver house but was forced to sell his interest in the Guston to pay
both Polly's and his own attorney fees.

Meanwhile during the years of his marriage and divorce, the
Red Mountain District was booming. Dividends paid to the stockholders of the Guston and the Yankee Girl were in the millions of
dollars. The National Bell, Congress, St. Paul, Paymaster, Barstow
and Treasury Tunnel were producing bountifully. It seemed the entire
district was a great body of ore. But between the early sale of the
Yankee Girl and his financial losses from the divorce, Andy Meldrum
was out of action.

In 1887 Otto Mears began the Silverton Railroad which was meant
to tap the Red Mountain mines, and by switchback and turntable
reach all the way to the Saratoga Mine, way down the mountain at
Ironton. But Otto Mears was unable to continue the railroad to Ouray
because of the canyon. Had he been able to do so he would have had
a railway that completely looped from Silverton to Ouray, Ridgway,
Telluride, Durango and back to Silverton. This led to a magnificent

Andy Meldrum was one of the original locators of the Yankee Girl Mine. It made him rich and began a huge boom on Red Mountain. This photograph shows the Yankee Girl at its peak. — COURTESY OF P. DAVID SMITH

dream for Andy. He proposed driving a 24,200 foot tunnel from Ironton to Telluride. The tunnel would be of sufficient size to permit its use as a railroad, and at the same time a sizable ditch within the tunnel would drain off the extensive water the bore was sure to encounter. This water would be used to power turbines which would furnish the electricity necessary to operate the tunnel. Undoubtedly Meldrum thought the tunnel would cross-cut valuable ore bodies, which by themselves, would pay dividends to the stockholders.

To obtain the funds necessary to drill the bore, Meldrum went to Scotland where he was favorably received by the Scottish bankers. He initially raised $25,000 and began the "Meldrum Tunnel" at both Telluride and Ironton. He had estimated the six-mile-long tunnel would take six years and cost $3,000,000. Within two years he anticipated the bore would strike rich veins and begin to pay for itself. And well it might have done so.

The Boer War cut off Meldrum's supply of capital, and the tunnel was never finished. Andy lived in near poverty and died in 1939 at the age of eighty-seven. Andy's tombstone records his birth year as 1851. In 1947- 48, the Idarado cut into the Meldrum Tunnel on the Telluride side. In its development it came across very rich ore deposits off the 2,850 feet driven by Meldrum from the Telluride side.

CHAPTER 10

THE LOST MINE AT MINERAL POINT

There's a lost bonanza near Mineral Point and it is as rich as the nearby fabulous Old Lout Mine. Perhaps it is only a few hundred feet from thousands of jeepers who pass annually on the Engineer Mountain trail. Today's explorers driving through Mineral Point are unlikely to know that this was a mining camp which at one time boasted of 1,000 inhabitants (but most likely might have actually only reached 300). It takes the most observant person to discover the one or two remaining foundations virtually submerged in the midst of the present-day swamp.

Some sixty years ago when a teenager, I spent most of a summer living in a tent near the London Mine (perhaps three-quarters of a mile from the site of Mineral Point) and suffered through daily rain showers which frequently carried ice and snow. We were engaged in unwatering a shaft about thirty-five feet in depth. It seemed that as fast as we winched out a barrel of water, the streams from the wet tundra refilled what we had dipped out. It was much like climbing a steep mountainside — two steps up and one step back.

At that time (in the '30s) the remains of the habitation at Mineral Point included perhaps six or seven deteriorated and collapsed cabins, including the wreckage of what we presumed to be a saloon with a false front and a two-story rickety (so rickety that even we teenagers were afraid to climb the broken stairs to the second floor) building which we assumed to be the remains of a hotel. Later research revealed that the name of the hotel was probably the Forest House — a most peculiar name when attached to a hotel in an area completely barren of trees!)

Today to get to Mineral Point, we leave the Million Dollar Highway at State Bridge where signs indicate the beginning of the fabulous Engineer jeep trail now called the Alpine Loop. Seven miles up that bumpy, chasm-edged road and just before the last steep climb to go up Engineer Pass, the remains of a great old mill stands - the San

Juan Chief. Just before coming abreast of the mill, a worn narrow road goes right through a rocky cut and leads to the swampy site of Mineral Point. This road is so muddy and soggy as to frequently prevent its use, but if followed, it eventually leads down to Animas Forks. A higher road circles around the camp, connects to the lower road and goes downward to Animas Forks and eventually Silverton. If you follow this now accepted route you will completely miss the site of Mineral Point.

According to the United States Geological Survey quadrangle map, the mining camp of Mineral Point was at approximately 11,500 feet in elevation. A 1946 Colorado Scientific Society paper defines Mineral Point as bounded by Poughkeepsie Gulch on the west, Engineer Mountain (13,218 ft.) on the north, the California Gulch divide (12,218 feet) on the southeast and Canadian Lake Basin on the south (a ridge of about 12,800 feet divides the lake from the flats of Mineral Point.) For some reason the Society omits mention of 13,274 foot Seigal Mountain to the east and 13,062 foot Houghton on the south. The same report describes the area of Mineral Point as ranging from 11,500 to 12,500 feet.

At one time (1877) Mineral Point was referred to as "the busiest camp in the San Juans." Its name was derived from several mineral veins which seemed to merge in a knob of quartz "fully 60 feet thick." The astounding Mastodon Vein can easily be seen by jeepers today, for it runs fifty feet wide "like a great wagon road" and goes in a straight line over mountains and through valleys.

The area was first prospected by Captain A.W. Burrows (who wisely spent his winters away from Mineral Point in the camp that was named after him), and Charles McIntyre in 1873, a year before Silverton and two years earlier than Ouray was founded. In fact it was from Mineral Point in 1875 that prospectors crept their way down the Uncompahgre Gorge to locate what is now the City of Ouray. Within a few months after the initial prospecting at Mineral Point the new camp was booming, and new discoveries seemed to be reported every day. In one in those early years the enthusiastic citizens changed the name to Mineral City. The first elected representative to the Colorado Territorial Legislature from the Silverton-Ouray area was McIntyre from Mineral Point. A post office was established on October 29, 1875.

Crofutt's 1885 guide reported that the "town consists of one store, a sawmill, several restaurants and saloons and the requisite number of log cabins for a population of 200." Improbable as it seems the *Ouray Times* in its 1877 coverage of Mineral Point, reported thirty-two miners spent the winter of 1876- 77 engaged in "mining operations of a considerable extent" at that high altitude, where snow must have been twelve or more feet deep.

The mines at Mineral Point must have appeared to be doing well. When the first newspaper was established at Animas Forks Bill Young (owner of the Mineral Point Mine with the same name) paid $500 for the first copy. Other major mines in the area were the Burrows, Mastodon, Vermillion, Dacotah, Ben Butler, Red Cloud and Yankton.

But it is the Old Lout and the lost mine somewhere near it that concerns us now. The Old Lout started in a stupid, awkward way as befitted its name. A shaft was dug down some 300 feet with no mineral of importance being found. The crew was ordered to quit, but one miner still having a charge of dynamite set it off as he left. The blast uncovered a body of high grade. The first carload was reported to have netted $8,000, and within a month $86,000 was realized. It is of a lost mine of such richness that we look for.

In 1935 when Ernest Miller was trying to decide if he wanted to add the Old Lout to his extensive holdings in the Lake Como-Poughkeepsie Gulch area (he did), I went with him into the Old Lout's Poughkeepsie Gulch tunnel which had at a later time been driven some 900 feet lower than the original collar of the shaft. At that time the shaft (the collar is at 11,557 feet) was in poor condition, and we did not attempt entry. It is an inclined shaft of about 500 feet and is reported to have six levels of workings. It was a fabulous source of high grade ore, $245,707.31 is reported as having been netted between 1884 and 1887. That sum is the equivalent of millions of dollars today. Water problems led to the determination to tap the vein at a lower altitude, with the subsequent tunnel draining the water and at the same time providing cheaper transportation than lifting the ore and rock out of a shaft.

The extensive dump at the tunnel indicates a successful and major operation, although our investigation indicated the true vein had never been tapped, but that the miners had drifted off on yet another valuable vein. Our reports showed the tunnel length at 1,865 feet with 1,700 more feet in drifts, cross cuts and raises. According to a government report the operation was abandoned in the nineties because of a disastrous snowslide and fire coupled with the major decline in silver prices in 1893. But we knew it had been extensively worked in later years, although we have no government reports. In fact operation of the Old Lout was the basis for the old ghost community of Poughkeepsie, which existed in the early years of the twentieth century. Poughkeepsie was located not far from where the road to Engineer and Mineral Point separates from the road up Poughkeepsie Gulch.

In our examination of the Old Lout we found considerable bad air, particularly in the drifts, which prevented our examination of them. We did determine the tunnel was at least 500 feet south of the shaft, and Miller suspected the tunnel had drifted off on the Forest vein (which was a mine 230 feet east of the Old Lout shaft). Thus the tunnel had never intersected the Old Lout vein. In addition to the bad air, that tunnel was wet, wet, wet!

It was far back in that wet tunnel that I had the worst underground scare I had ever experienced. We were so far back that the only the light was from our carbide lights. Suddenly the whole tunnel seemed to vibrate from a crashing rock fall. We abandoned our examination and headed back out, fearful with every step we would find our exit blocked by that rock fall and knowing full well that no one knew we had entered the Old Lout. As the car was back at our tent, a mile or two away, that would not offer any searchers a clue as to our whereabouts. We might well be entombed forever. It turned out that the rock fall must have been in one of the side drifts and did not endanger our way out of the main tunnel. We never went back.

Reports on mining in the San Juans are fragmentary at best and non-existent too often. While the government reports contain no information on the Old Lout being worked around the turn-of-the-century, we know from newspapers that it was, and we know that James Herring was one of the miners. Herring was highly respected by his friends at Mineral Point as well as in Ouray. He came from England in 1868 at the age of fifteen. By 1880 he was at Mineral Point and was part owner of the Solid Democrat Mine and superintendent of the Red Cloud. The mine was one of the major producers of the hey-day of Mineral Point. Boilers and other surface machinery are still located at the Red Cloud.

In 1883 when he was age thirty, Herring married Mary Beck of Lockhaven, Pennsylvania where the Herrings settled when they came from England. Mary Beck came to the San Juans to marry Herring and the ceremony took place at Mineral Point with considerable publicity as the "highest wedding ceremony in the country." A wedding picture in possession of the Ouray County Historical Society shows a handsome and charming couple. The reception and wedding dinner were held at the Red Cloud Mine, with everyone from Mineral Point and the surrounding country being invited.

As we have said, winters at Mineral Point were severe so the couple settled in Ouray and bought a house at 629 Fourth Street, across from the present Community Center. Like all prospectors and miners, Herring was sure he was about to strike it rich, and because his prospect was at Mineral Point, he went to work at the Old Lout Mine as an engineer. The Old Lout was near enough to his claim that he could work on his hoped-for bonanza during every free moment. Each evening he would hurry off to work rather than eating with the crew, and after darkness had come he would return to the Old Lout to eat left-overs in the kitchen. According to the other miners he was secretive and refused to allow others to accompany him to his claim.

Heavy winters and dangerous snowslides caused the Old Lout to close every autumn, and in the fall of 1901 the mine closed down as usual. Herring stayed on to work his claim. It was on November 1, 1901 that he finally struck a fabulously rich bonanza. Having proved to his satisfaction that it was not simply a pocket, he sampled the vein and carrying his discovery, took off down the seven mile trail to Ouray to show his samples and share his good news with Mary. But he had delayed too long.

Herring was overtaken on the seven mile journey by a wet snowstorm and by the time he reached Ouray he was shivering and coughing badly. Mary put him to bed, called the doctor and fussed over him. He told her of the bonanza that is "richer than the Old Lout," and the samples under his bed proved his tale. On November 7, 1902 James Herring died in the bed that covered the rich ore samples. The pneumonia had activated the "miners con" he had developed over the years of working in mines while drilling without water to dampen the rock dust. Today we call this consumption silicosis. James Herring was housebound until his death. He was fifty years old.

Mary Herring did hire men to explore the Solid Democrat, but they found no evidence of recent work, so that probably was not his bonanza. She had failed to write down the indefinite directions he told her as to the location of his bonanza, and the men she hired had no luck in locating the mine. We can guess that the workings–either a tunnel or shaft –must not have left a large dump, for one man is unlikely to have accomplished much. We can only guess it must have been fairly near the Old Lout for him to have been able to work there almost every evening. But where?

Possibly there are two "lost mines" on Mineral Point. One would be the Old Lout itself, for the lower tunnel never encountered the Old Lout vein.

As to the other - well, somewhere on the sodden Mineral Point area is a very rich mine, in a shallow cut, just waiting for someone to scrape aside the accumulations of ninety-five years of rock dirt and vegetation to find the rich bonanza that awaits.

The Old Lout Mine, shown in this photo, was a valuable property, but an even greater discovery may be nearby—waiting to be relocated. — AUTHOR'S COLLECTION

CHAPTER 11

BOOTLEG WAS THE ECONOMY

The " Great Experiment" of the Eighteenth Amendment known as Prohibition began before such a great effort to our way of living could impress my infant mind. However the days of Prohibition certainly influenced my youthful life. My family was a staunch prohibition supporter. Grandmother LaRoche, who lived with us, was one of the original WTCU crusaders when she lived in Wilmington, Illinois. Wilmington was a key point on the Illinois-Michigan canal, and Grandfather was a captain on the canal. In both Wilmington and nearby Joliet the rough rivermen enjoyed the saloons and the houses with available girls. Amazingly I never heard of the women of that day who organized the Woman's Christian Temperance Union as having taken action against the houses of prostitution, but they did swing a mighty axe against the doors and bars of the saloons. Grandmother did this at least once before Grandfather put a stop to such actions.

In Ouray, she and mother were members of the WTCU. So our household was on the side of the Eighteenth Amendment. As aware as they were of the stills and open selling of liquor in those days of prohibition, they took no overt action in opposition to what was going on in our city. And plenty was going on. A friend of the family left me a note about the coming of prohibition in Telluride and the scenes in the street of the last night it was legal to sell whiskey. It must have been quite a night, with a sizable portion of the inhabitance getting thoroughly drunk. The next day he went back to work at the Liberty Bell Mine high above Telluride. When he came back to town two weeks later, he was astonished to see the saloons were operating just as they had for all the years Telluride had existed. The same was true, I am sure, in Silverton. Ouray's Main Street, where perhaps thirteen saloons had been operating until prohibition came, now had only three or four remaining open.

As a small boy going with Grandmother down Main Street I could never understand why we crossed and recrossed the street so

Bootleggers made their "booze" just about any place. The author's mother discovered the watchman of their mill. (the Gold Crown shown in this photo) made his own special brew.
— Courtesy of P. David Smith

many times. Of course I now know it was because she wouldn't walk in front of a saloon, which forced us to cross to the other side of the street. The "boarding houses for girls" (as so listed by the United States Census) and the numerous saloons did offer some difficulties to the proper ladies of the town. They made every effort to pretend those places did not exist.

A daughter of Louis King, an influential businessman, told me of her arrival in Ouray near the turn of the century. She and her sister were met at the train station by a driver of one of her grandfathers' carriages and were driven to her grandfather's home. It was evening, and the houses and streets were lighted. When deposited at her grandfather's home, she greeted him by asking if he couldn't put some of those lovely red lights on his porch that she had seen as they had driven along.

Making whiskey was an important part of income of those prohibition days. Mining was in a vast downturn and Ouray was depressed ten years before the Wall Street collapse of 1929. So the operation of stills was a financial necessity. The local bottling works put aside bottling soft drinks, and bottled booze instead, slapping a

Ouray label on every bottle. Liquor runners went down the Uncompahgre Valley, over to Gunnison, across Monarch Pass down to Salida. There another set of runners took the load through the mountains to the plains, and a third group of runners carried the load to Kansas City where the Ouray label was in high demand because of its fine quality. Every effort was made locally to keep the quality high.

My first job away from Colorado was working on a census of agriculture in Washington, D.C.. When they considered the agricultural census of Ouray, the "experts" were shocked at the price that corn was reported to be worth - much higher than the rest of the United States. I was able to tell them that in Ouray we rated the corn yield, not by bushels, but by gallons.

Of course there were raids by the prohibition agents. But few were ever successful, because the routes into Ouray were so limited. If the agent came from Denver, they would arrive by train at Ridgway, secure a car and head either for Ouray or Telluride. If they came by car from Grand Junction, they also had to pass through Ridgway. The telephone was faster than autos, and long before the agents' arrival the bottles disappeared from the premises where they were dispensed.

In Telluride one druggist kept his stock on a wooden shelf under the soda fountain counter. The shelf was supported by a stick. If by some mischance agents arrived without notice, all the druggist had to do was knock the stick out from under the shelf so that the bottles fell and broke on the cement below and drained into a depression that poured into the sewer. Another movement of the druggist's foot covered the depression with a plank of wood. If the agent was wise enough to move the plank, all he could find was broken glass.

The "feds" had information that one of the big stills in Ouray was located in Powell's Grocery. The grocery was raided repeatedly, and the men sitting in front of the great pot-bellied stove that stood in the center of the store were occasionally searched. Look as they did, the "feds" never came upon the still. The still was actually inside the big pot-bellied stove, and when the agents were reported as coming a fire was built in the stove, and men came to congregate around its warmth. The "feds" never guessed the subterfuge.

Before my father's death he had built, or rather rebuilt, the old Grand View Mill, just below Ouray to handle ore from the mines he was interested in. The mill never operated, because the night it was finished it burned to the ground. Still there was some heavy machinery there that had value, so mother hired a watchman to live at the mill. Word came to her that the watchman was making whiskey. Concerned that if raided she would be held responsible for the still, she walked down to the mill and investigated. The watchman pleasantly showed her around the various remaining shacks, and then with a leer suggested they might go into the shack in which he lived and enjoy a cup of coffee. The leer did it; mother backed off and scurried back to town, and the watchman kept making his bootleg in his living shack.

Ed Washington, a respected black businessman and gambler, operated the gambling house above where the Silver Nugget restaurant is now located. Washington was the gentleman who sent a pair of alligators to Ouray. They lived in a warm water pool near the hot springs pool for many years. Washington had found that spending the winters in warm Louisiana was important to his aches. His gambling brought him enough funds that he could afford to spend winter in Louisiana. It was on one of these trips that he thought of sending the alligators to Ouray. They came as a surprise, and the mayor sent a telegram to him in Louisiana asking him what to feed them. Washington replied with a telegram of a single word; "Pickaninnies". But now to get back to the subject. Of course Washington carried a bit of the liquid which encouraged men to enlarge their bets. Somehow an agent got word (perhaps from an unlucky patron) that Washington had some of that banned substance in his hall. The "feds" found the illegal hooch in a raid. Washington was arrested and brought to trial. He never went to prison as he was found not guilty when his attorney, Carl Seigfred, pointed out Washington was in Louisiana at the time of the raid and could have had no knowledge of any whiskey being served. Why, Ed Washington was greatly surprised that the "feds" had found bootleg in his hall!

Ever since the 1890s when the southern Europeans arrived to work in the mines, wine-making was big business in Ouray. After prohibition came the big wine vat, which was located adjoining what we now call the Coachlight, was carried by Carl Seigfred down to the Portland where he placed it as a water storage tank. It is still there, although the current owners of the pleasant bungalow now receive their water from a utility.

Prohibition didn't stop the making of wine in the bathrooms and cellars of half of Ouray's population who had origins in the Austrian-Italian area of Europe. In the spring these industrious people gathered dandelions which were pressed to make a very delicious dandelion wine. In the fall the Cascade Grocery imported from two to four boxcars of grapes for eating, of course. But a good portion of Ouray's populous enjoyed wine all winter.

Finding stills was a lot of fun for the members of my gang. We found one in the covered waterway that led for several blocks from the Uncompahgre River to the Munn Sampling Works. At one time its water turned the wheels of the grinding equipment, but for many years no water had passed through the tunnel. Sure enough, there, a block from either end, we found a still. There was another one above Oak Street along the pipeline that carried hot water from the springs below Box Canyon. Harry Lewis, a black man who lived on the hillside not far from us, had a still in the tunnel at old Al Temp, about a half mile out of town. My sister found a still one day in Portland Creek under a rock overhang just a mite away from Ohio Park. It scared the daylights out of her, for while she and a friend were looking at the still they heard a horse coming. They had scarcely found a place to hide before a rider arrived and spent the next little while suspiciously looking for an invader. When he left the two girls scurried home to safety. And so it went.

The house next door to the county courthouse handled a good sized operation. And even the sheriff operated a still in the jail! The "feds" caught that one, and Sheriff Laird spent the last years of his term doing time in Leavenworth at a different kind of term than he was elected to.

CHAPTER 12 ✹

THE MYSTERY OF THE COPPER MINING TOOLS

Lake Como, at an elevation of 12,300 feet, was the site of an intriguing and amazing discovery in 1878. John M. Stuart, a Scot, had been sent from Great Britain to the exciting new mining fields in the San Juans. Following reports of rich mining prospects in the Poughkeepsie vicinity, he began mining explorations on the banks of Lake Como. What he discovered remains one of the most interesting, if not profitable, finds in the San Juans.

But first a word about Lake Como. It is reported to be a volcanic crater and to be bottomless. As a teenager back in 1936, I set out with my brother and an older companion to find out if this was true. We built a raft of boards and beams. We did not question where and how that lumber came to be there. There were the remains of a lot of old mine buildings and mine structures in that high, high land back then in the 1930s.

At that time the remains of power lines ran every which way. Some of the poles led to Silverton, some to Lake City, but most came off of the main lines and went to old abandoned mines. One set of lines led into Lake Como; why we didn't stop to consider.

There was an old mine dump that emptied into the lake, and it was from that point that we launched our thoroughly unwieldy raft. We appropriated the power line running to the mine at the edge of the lake, attached a large rock to the wire and set out to the middle of the lake. Once there we rolled the rock off the raft (almost upsetting it in the process, and if we had been dumped into that freezing water I doubt we could have survived). The rock pulled on the wire and went down and down, and it just kept going. We must have had at least 500 feet of wire attached, and when the end of that wire slid over the edge of the raft, it was still sinking at a high speed. How deep is Lake Como? Let's just say it is DEEP.

The first recorded discovery of Lake Como and the headwaters of Poughkeepsie Gulch was in August of 1873. Two pioneers of the San Juans, George Howard and Rueben James McNutt, were on an exploration trip when they came across the lake. The story of George Howard and his place in the San Juans deserves a chapter or a book by itself. Briefly, Howard was a part of the 1860 gold rush to the San Juans (referred to as the San Juan Humbug by Denver's *Rocky Mountain News*). He was not a part of the original Baker group but came independently via Cochetopa Pass, the Gunnison River, the Uncompahgre River, then through the site of the present town of Ouray and via the Red Mountains to Baker's Park. He was adventurous and may well have spent more time on exploration than in panning for gold. On one of these exploratory ventures in 1861 he left Baker's Park and traveled west to the Dolores and San Miguel Rivers. He turned from the San Miguel and headed back east through what is known today as the Howard Fork. In 1870 he was among the first to return to the San Juans. Everyone of the hundreds in the Baker venture had left in 1861 or 1862 because of disappointment with their efforts to find gold using panning and placer methods or by news of the impending Civil War. Howard's impact on the subsequent activities on Baker's Park resulted in Howardsville being named for him. Howardsville was the first county seat in Western Colorado and the site of the first court in the San Juans.

After the settlement at Ouray began in 1875 the usual route for traveling between Silverton and Ouray was via Cement Creek, Lake Como and Poughkeepsie. The large veins and outcroppings in the Lake Como area attracted attention, and soon claims criss-crossed the mountains. It also attracted the attention of outside investors including Leadville's H.A.W. Tabor.

Stuart began exploration in 1878 on the west shore of the lake. What led him to dig in this particular spot we will never know. But soon his men uncovered an old tunnel. Clearing out the tunnel they advanced into the mountain over 100 feet, and there they found old copper mining tools! Considerable evidence exists that the Spanish were in the area. Would they have used copper mining tools? I think not, for Spain was famous for the production of fine steel. The Ute Indians did not mine. Who then? The Aztecs? Mayans? The *Ouray Times* reported that Stuart promised to investigate the copper tools' origin. But our tale ends there, for there are no further reports as to what he discovered. A good guess would be that he forwarded the tools to the British Museum (the widely traveled English sent to the museum all sorts of unusual items they found in their journeys). Some years back I wrote to the British Museum to see if they had any record of the copper tools found on the shore of Lake Como. I never received a reply. That the tools might have been Spanish seems out of the question. The Spanish were past masters at the art of making steel and iron and would never have thought of using soft copper for mining. Did the tunnel and the tools antedate the Spanish, and if so who were the miners? Could the origins have been Aztec or Mayan? Truly, this is a most intriguing mystery.

Lake Como sits deep, deep down in a basin at the head of Poughkeepsie Gulch. It is centered in a very mineral rich area and was the site of some of the earliest San Juan discoveries.
— AUTHOR'S PHOTO

This is the site on the edge of Lake Como where the mine existed which the author describes. It is now probably covered over by loose rock. — AUTHOR'S FAMILY COLLECTION

CHAPTER 13

THE STORY OF THE THREE POUGHKEEPSIES

Lake Como always fascinated me. When I was a small boy Mother used to tell of riding horseback to reach the lake and the beautiful blue water. Lake Como is at a high altitude, 12,300 feet, with tall mountains surrounding. The Lake is in an old volcano crater, or so I have always been told. Melting snow on the surrounding mountainsides keep it filled. I have never seen any indication of fish life.

It was only lately when Allen Nossaman issued his multi-volume book "Many More Mountains," that I learned about the camp of Poughkeepskie that at one time was located on the banks of Lake Como. From his account of the camp of Poughkeepsie I suspect that we launched our raft from the dump of the tunnel that John M. Stuart found, and the materials we used in building that raft sixty years ago may have been the remains of the community he writes about.

There is a lot of confusion as to the site of Poughkeepsie. I suspect there were at least three camps that carried the name - none of them big enough to be labeled a town. I have been shown a site high on a mountainside above Lake Como in Alaska Basin as being where Poughkeepsie was located — perhaps. A much later and far longer lasting Poughkeepsie was located at the fork where Poughkeepsie Gulch joins the beginnings of the Uncompahgre River. This is very near the point where the jeep trail into Poughkeepsie leaves the road going to Engineer Pass. Perhaps twenty-five years ago I told an acquaintance of this location, and the next time I went by the lovely glen it had been all dug up by bottle hunters searching for loot discarded from the saloon and restaurant – a coincidence?

I was told back in the early 1930s by our family friend Ernest Miller that this Poughkeepsie existed in the 1890s and lasted into the early part of the twentieth century. It consisted of a few cabins or houses, a store, and a combined eating house and saloon, where his mother was cook. There at the turn of the century, he spent his boyhood.

This Poughkeepsie never had a post office but did have a mail tree. This was a tree that stood near the main trail that led down to Ouray. There was a hollow in the tree and in that hollow mail was left to be carried to Ouray by whomever might be traveling that way. Such a tree or rock was in common usage throughout the San Juans by those living far from post offices. Such a rock is reported by Nossaman to have been located near Wagon Wheel Gap, and I know of a similar one located far up on the road we now call Imogene Pass.

One of the mule skinners down at Johnnie Donald's stable used to keep us boys enthralled and in stitches as he told about trying to pick up the mail. He was leading his pack train down from the Upper Camp Bird when he stopped to pick up the mail left at that post office rock. He found he was so frozen to the saddle, that in his efforts to dismount, his saddle turned on him and he found himself hanging down under the belly of his horse still frozen to the saddle.

But somehow I've gotten away from the subject of Lake Como. The mining efforts of Superintendent Stuart and the British Consuls Mining Company which he represented, brought a number of miners to live in that high, extremely harsh area near Lake Como. The Columbia Mine, also by 1878, was shipping ore to the Greene Smelter in Silverton. The infamous Horace Tabor with his new found millions from mining in Leadville also moved into the San Juans while getting his probably illegal divorce from Augusta to marry Baby Doe. Tabor bought the Alaska, Red Rogers, Saxon, and Amador mines, all of which showed rich silver ore and were deemed worthy of development. By 1879 perhaps a couple of hundred men were expected to spend the winter working on these and other properties.

With 200 men captive for the winter at that remote location and unable to get to Silverton for supplies, entertainment or liquor, an entrepreneur built a store, obtained a liquor license and was granted a post office. Thus it became "the highest post office in the United States" at 12,300 feet. We can say it was very high. The San Juan County commissioners called the small community Lake Como, but the post office listed it as Poughkeepsie. In 1880 the census actually listed only one family of three in residence. By the end of 1881 the post office was discontinued, and Lake Como's Poughkeepsie disappeared. It probably did have the distinction of beings the highest post office ever located at an actual community. There may have been as high or higher post offices for mines, but not for a community with family and children present!

The Lake Como - Alaska Basin was just too remote, too high, and too difficult to mine successfully. All transportation had to be by foot or burro, making the shipment of ore out and supplies in just too expensive. It wasn't until well after World War II and the intrusion of the four-wheeled jeeps, that access by wheel became possible and then only for a limited few summer months.

I am convinced that one day a major mine will be developed around the fantastic veins that interlace at Lake Como. It will have to be a different concept of mining than those of the original pioneers — it will have to be a deep tunnel to avoid the harsh climate. That same summer when we tried to find the bottom of Lake Como, we also tried to find out if any existing tunneling could be used to reach the mineralization at Lake Como. In that year (1936) the Bagley (or Frisco- use which ever promotional name you wish) Tunnel still had a watchman, a mill in such condition that it could be used for an immediate start-up, and a tunnel with power and electric motors. The watchman lived in Animas Forks, perhaps a mile further down the road, and with a small amount of interchange we were able to have the power in the tunnel turned on and take a motor car for a survey. Originally, this was started as the Bonanza Tunnel and later was commonly called the Mineral Point Tunnel in 1877. Pratt was one of the first to use the new-fangled steam drills and other modern (for that day) techniques. He succeeded in driving the tunnel 1,000 of the 6,000 feet projected. The intention was to tap the mines at Mineral Point at the lower altitude. At that point his backers gave up, because he never did cross any major veins. Later the Bagley Tunnel developers went straight back for another couple of thousand feet, before their backers gave up. They had the same result, at least in our investigation we found no important mineralization. Still it hadn't reached the Mineral Point mines. It did not lead toward the Lake Como mineral fields. While at 11,200 feet the mine was a thousand feet lower than Lake Como. At that altitude it still meant a considerable fight with the snow and elements. So we forgot this as a possibility.

I was astonished in returning to the San Juans after WWII to find the mine stripped of the equipment that was in good operating condi-

This is an example of the abandoned debris and mining equipment that littered the area of the town of Poughkeepsie above Lake Como in the 1930s. — AUTHOR'S FAMILY COLLECTION

tion only a few years before. The great mill structure that had housed an operating mill had been busted wide open, probably by dynamite, to pull the machinery out to become scrap metal used in the war.

I have two further comments. In the mid-1930s, there was still a considerable amount of the remains of mining at Lake Como and the Alaska Basin and still a couple of complete buildings at Mineral Point. By the mid-1950s, after World War II, I returned to the San Juans to find almost all evidence of human presence had disappeared. Machinery had been ripped from the mountainsides, and old mill buildings destroyed. This was done to pull out the machinery to be sold as scrap for the high prices brought about by the war effort. Old buildings sagged and collapsed under the weight of snow, and sheepherders burned up the lumber and tore down structures to build fires. Still as late as 1959 a large bunkhouse stood at the Amador. The building collapsed in the early 1960s, the victim of savage San Juan winters. Only a few boards remain at Alaska Basin's Poughkeepsie and nothing at Lake Como. The combined efforts of man and weather have destroyed much of the heritage of the San Juans.

The second comment — what terrible headaches the men must have had in the morning- after-the-night-before drinking at the 12,300 foot Lake Como saloon!

CHAPTER 14 🌿

ROSE'S CABIN

When I first saw Rose's Cabin in the 1930s, it was still a most impressive log building. The three of us kids didn't go inside, although it was obviously vacant, several "No Trespassing" signs kept us from entering. I've often regretted not having done so, for Rose's Cabin has always seemed to me to have been one of the most impossible outposts in the San Juan mining country. It was located in Henson Creek just at timberline, at the edge of that great, almost barren area known as American Flats. The road from Lake City passes Rose's Cabin, crosses a bit of American Flats and several mines, the most significant being the Frank Haugh, then winds over Engineer Pass to access Mineral Point. From there the traveler may go to Animas Forks, Eureka, Silverton or Ouray.

Quite logically Rose's Cabin relates to Lake City. There was easy access to that mining town as compared to terrible trails to either Silverton or Ouray. But to those of us involved in Mineral Point, Poughkeepsie and Lake Como, it was only a skip and a jump over Engineer Mountain. Granted that trail was horrendous, but when you are young and filled with a fascination of that high country, the perils of such a trail offered little resistance. But before I go further, the trail at that time over Engineer Pass was not where the current jeep road crosses today; the jeep road is for sissies as compared to the old trail. Today Rose's Cabin, or rather the site of the cabin, is an easy passenger car trip from Lake City. The road up Henson Creek in the 1880s was something else. (Henson Creek was named for Henry Henson, a member of the legendary Baker parties of 1860. He returned to the San Juans in 1871 and was one of those who discovered the great Ute and Ulay Mines of Lake City. This discovery precipitated the founding of Lake City, and appropriately, he was elected in 1876 as the first state senator representing the San Juans.)

Corydon Rose arrived in the San Juans in 1874 much later than Henson. When he crossed over from the Animas River drainage, Rose must have fallen in love with the country he found, for when he descended from the high alpine meadows to the protective spruce forest marking timberline, he promptly stopped and began felling trees to make his log cabin. Strategically located between Lake City and Engineer Pass, he soon found that many people making that journey sought his cabin as a way station. Accordingly two years later, he added the first of many additions and set himself up as an innkeeper.

Not only did he serve as a way stop for travelers, but his cabin became the center of a thriving community serving the needs of prospectors and miners of that era. Rose's Cabin was occupied all year round. A large stable was built and a significant forwarding and packing business existed. But the winters were frightful.

In 1878 Rose and his prospecting partner, Charles Schafer, were working their nearby claim and living there in a small cabin. A snowslide smashed into the cabin injuring the two men, Rose nearly fatally. That same day a teamster driving over the Engineer road was carried 1,000 feet down the side of Engineer Mountain and was buried up to his neck. He was saved by a nearby miner who heard his desperate calls for help. A day later Charles Curtis was killed by a slide as he journeyed up Henson Creek expecting to spend the night at Rose's Cabin.

The same year, but a winter later in December 1878, Nicholas Lytle and his companion Jackson Gregory were working at their claim on Dolly Varden Mountain. They had left the claim to get supplies at Rose's Cabin and were returning when the snowslide hit them.

Lytle had a most colorful history — a California miner in the gold rush of 1849, a Pony Express rider in the Utah division, and a part of the Pike's Peak Gold Rush of 1859. When the Civil War began he returned to California and enlisted as a private. Part of the time he fought Indians near Tucson and suffered a broken arm from a war club wielded by an Apache. At the conclusion of his military service he traveled to Central and South America on a prospecting trip and for awhile operated a cattle ranch in Kansas.

Prospecting drew him back to Colorado, and Lytle joined the 1876 rush to Lake City and subsequently located the Chipmunk Claim above Rose's Cabin. He took as a partner Jackson Gregory, who had a wife and eight children living in Capitol City, between Rose's Cabin and Lake City.

Both the mail carrier and the miners at the Copper Chance, across the valley from the Chipmunk, heard the December slide come down but assumed that the two men had reached their cabin safely. Two days later, after seeing no activity at the Chipmunk, the Copper Chance miners walked down to Rose's Cabin to see if the two had by chance returned there; they hadn't.

Digging for the unfortunate men went on for a number of days. Gregory was found under four feet of snow, but Lytle was ten feet under solidly packed white stuff. The bodies were carried up to Gregory's Cabin in Capitol City. The Rev. George Darley conducted the funeral services with both men's coffins placed side by side and Gregory's wife with a child at her breast and seven other stair-stepped children surrounding them. Gregory was buried by the Masons at Lake City in the Masonic Cemetery, Lytle by the Odd Fellows in the City Cemetery. Reverend Darley assures us that the men of the community cared for the widow and her flock for the rest of the winter, but we do not know in the years that followed how she could possibly have cared for her eight little ones.

Some years later in 1882 a murder took place in Rose's Cabin. Two men who were engaged in an all-night poker game came to blows. Big Joe Nevins struck Andy MacLauchan a glancing blow in the forehead with an axe. Andy in return shot Nevins, "a rough character who deserved his fate." Nobody helped the dying Nevins. MacLauchan turned himself in to Lake City authorities, and the killing was held to be self-defense and justified.

After the mining boom in the American Flats, Poughkeepsie, and Mineral Point ended, Rose's Cabin was abandoned. A group of hunters and vacationers bought the cabin and remodeled it for their purposes. I presume it was still in their hands when I first saw the "No Trespassing" signs in the 1930s. One account of the later years tells of the experiences of four young ladies hiking from Mesa Verde who stopped at Rose's cabin and spent the night. The caretaker offered them a wide choice of rooms and lowered the beds from the ceiling where they had been hoisted for the winter to keep the bedding and mattresses safe from pack rats. They were most taken with the old inn, and one of the four girls who had always insisted she would be a spinster school teacher, consented she would be willing to marry one of the stockholders who owned the inn if she could spend her summers there. The caretaker had a string of pack mules and carried the girls on down to Lake City.

The last time we stopped to explore at the site of the little community about the only significant item we saw was a rusting old safe which must have been the "bank" Corydon Rose used to hold valuables for the miners who centered their lives around Rose's Cabin. I wonder if that old safe still lies on the wet ground, or has some souvenir hunter taken away that last remnant of a most unlikely center of habitation?

This early photograph of Rose's Cabin shows its early beginnings as a simple log cabin. The cabin is named after Corydon Rose, a man not a woman. — AUTHOR'S COLLECTION

CHAPTER 15 🌿

MAIL FROM HOME

To the men on America's mining frontier in the 1870s and 1880s, a letter from home was greatly anticipated. Even if you had no one back home to write to you, the day when mail was to arrive was a day to join the others waiting in a bond of fellowship. Even without a letter, someone who received a newspaper might be willing to share it with you. While the lucky recipients of letters were enjoying them, others might be joining in reading the latest news which was sure to be a week or more out of date. Often a newspaper would be stripped apart and the individual pages passed around to be read; of course all the pages would eventually be gathered together and the entire newspaper carried home by the one receiving it.

If the mail didn't arrive on the scheduled day, the cluster of disappointed men would break up and go back to faraway cabins, to return the next day. The unfortunate prospector who expected or hoped for a letter that didn't arrive might slip away to attempt to find solace in his lonely cabin. In a mining area like the San Juans, the cabins were often great distances apart, for they were located on the claims scattered and remote from each other.

Mail was erratic in its delivery, being sent through distribution points miles and usually days way. In the San Juans the mail usually came through Del Norte, seventy miles distant. Weather had a great deal to do with the irregularity, as it impacted the carrier who had to travel those long miles. Frequently the government made no effort to deliver to the outlying post offices. These places became dependent upon the volunteer efforts of someone in the community. Sometimes as in Mineral Point, a purse was made up to pay the volunteer.

Amazingly the postal system was far more responsive to their customers then than is the bureaucratic monolith of today. Post offices were established in those years (1870-1890) in tiny, newly established and remote communities. Today's post office officials would sneer at the suggestion of establishing such small post offices.

So it was in 1875 when Ouray had a population of thirteen and was the most westerly community in all of Colorado. Yet a post office was established, and a postmaster designated. Now getting the mail to that mountain-bound grouping of three cabins was another problem. If the thirteen wanted mail one of them would have to lace on snow shoes or skis and fight ten to twenty-five foot drifts of snow and cross 11,000 to 12,500 foot passes to carry mail out or bring mail in.

Surprisingly Ouray was not as unlikely a location for a post office as were others that were established. At least the Ouray post office, as it turned out, was to signal the beginning of a permanent community. Although the first post office lasted only over the winter, it was reestablished in a month, never to be again discontinued.

Then there was Jennison. Located in the Rio Grande side of the Continental Divide, it was named for a young couple who had taken over some rough log buildings called the Carr Camp. As far as I know the Jennisons were the only residents. If it wasn't for a segment of the Hayden Survey that passed that way in 1875 we would know nothing of that young couple who located in a wilderness far from others. The Jackson division of the Hayden Survey reported Irene Jennison to be a lovely young woman. Charlie Jennison, her husband, had come to Colorado in 1863 and married Irene in Georgetown seven years later. He then served successfully as town marshal in the eastern plain town of Kit Carson when it was rough and woolly. The couple moved into the abandoned Carr's Cabins with the announced intention of providing a hotel and eating house for the travelers going and coming from Animas Country.

The last outpost of civilization was Del Norte, many miles away on the Rio Grande River. Possibly the reason for granting a post office to the Jennisons was that their cluster of two or three log cabins was the "jumping off" place when leaving the Rio Grande drainage to cross the Continental Divide and descend to the new settlements at Howardsville and Silverton. Two possible routes faced travelers when they left the Jennisons. One was over Cunningham Pass and the other over Stony Pass. Either were simply horrendous. Cunningham remains nothing but a trail even today, but a very rough jeep road now follows the terribly difficult Stony Pass road which the pioneers scratched out until it became the main artery of supply to the Animas River mining camps. The Jennisons were granted the post office in January of 1875 with

Charles Jennison appointed postmaster. But Jennison was killed in a shooting in Del Norte in early March, and in April Irene became postmistress until December of that year when the post office was withdrawn. It was later reinstated for a couple more years under the same name when a different family bought Irene's interest out. Then it was discontinued forever. When the Jackson party stopped for a meal Irene told them her husband was fishing and would return at any moment. The truth was Charlie was already dead, and the white lie she told was an attempt to protect herself. We wish we could tell what happened to the widow Irene. If she was as lovely as Jackson tells, she surely was remarried soon in that "woman-short" country.

A post office with a more logical reason for being was at Niegoldstown. Where Jennison had marked the beginning of the trail over Cunningham and Stony passes on the east side of the Continental Divide, Niegoldstown was located at the beginning of the ascent on the western side. Where the Jennisons had been a single couple living alone, Niegoldstown was a small mining community.

The camp was founded by four brothers named Niegold, together with a half brother. All came from Germany although two had been in the states for some time before immigrating to the San Juans. These two were pioneer arrivals in the San Juans, and by 1874, had located the Philadelphia which turned out to be an amazingly rich silver claim. They sent for the other three brothers, and soon several log cabins were erected and perhaps twenty to thirty men employed. Mill equipment and a sawmill were purchased and shipped over difficult Stony Pass; the rushing water of Stony Creek powered both mills. The sawmill made improved log structures possible, and the brothers erected a little store to supply both their small community and travelers who had to pass through their settlement to go over either Stony or Cunningham Passes. Soon a small log hotel also was built. The store and hotel took the pressure off the Niegolds to provide food and shelter at their own expense to the considerable number of travelers. It was quite logical for a post office to be established, and this was done in 1878.

The brothers must have been quite cultured, for they sent away for a grand piano. How that was carried over Stony Pass on the back of mules has never been explained. The piano was used to provide concerts and as accompaniment for an opera the brothers presented, reportedly in costume and wigs.

With their imported wine and music the brothers lived a life in much contrast to that of most of the men in the San Juans in those early years. Unfortunately, the rich pocket of ore in the Philadelphia played out, and by 1881 the post office was discontinued. Three years later in 1884 an avalanche destroyed all of the buildings of the community. But shed no tears for the Niegold brothers; for although losing their settlement, piano and the rich ore of the Philadelphia, after a period of paucity they found the even richer Old One Hundred Mine. There they lived on with the style they had enjoyed twenty years earlier at Niegoldstown. If there is even a nail remaining from this original camp we have been unable to find it, and the exact location eludes us.

The earliest request for mail service into the San Juans was by Charles Baker, that egocentric who still today defies understanding. In a letter written in 1860, he sought mail service for the 300 to 500 people located at Animas City with many more arriving daily. Probably these figures were an exaggeration, but certainly such a community did exist, and it was reported in 1869 that thirty to forty cabins still stood, and that more had earlier been burned by Indians after its abandonment in 1861. Of course nothing came of that 1860 proposal, as all members of the Baker parties left the San Juans the year following.

The so called "Baker Party" was really a number of parties who heard in "civilized" Denver (which was only a couple of years old) that Baker had found a new gold field in the remote San Juans. Wanting to be on the ground floor for this new bonanza, various parties headed to the San Juans, even as the winter of 1860 approached. There are reports that as many as 2,000 may have started out; but certainly the number arriving must have been much fewer. Many lived during the winter at Animas City in log cabins which they had built themselves. The *Rocky Mountain News* called the whole affair the "San Juan Humbug," and the disillusioned gold seekers abandoned the search and the San Juans early in the summer of 1861.

It was in 1869 that small groups of prospectors again entered the San Juans. All who entered the San Juans at this time prospected only in the summer and left when winter came. Nevertheless by 1873 enough men had entered into what was to become the Silverton area that their grumbles over the cost of securing mail began to reach Washington. What mail service existed was by way of travelers who went back and forth between Del Norte and Howardsville (the main camp at that time). The miners paid from $0.25 to $0.50 over the actual postage for this unofficial service. In the summer of 1874 the first post office in Western Colorado was established at Howardsville, but there was still no official mail service to this outpost. In fact even Del Norte was experiencing difficulty in receiving mail. Deliveries to that village had dropped to once a week. Such mail as came to Howardsville still came by the luck of whomever was going or coming and was willing to carry letters.

For the first time that winter a number of people stayed in the Animas River communities of Howardsville and newly established Silverton. As many as fifty men may have wintered in Silverton, but the number was much smaller in Howardsville. One who remained because of his duties as county clerk was John Ufford. He assumed the duties of postmaster from W.W. Randall. Randall operated a store together with a saloon and the post office. Randall, like most of the others of that high elevation, left for the winter for somewhere lower and with less snow. He left County Clerk Ufford in charge of not only the post office, but of forty gallons of whiskey, with instructions it all should be sold that winter. Ufford couldn't bring himself to charge the men wintering with him and convivially enjoyed drinking it with those who chanced to stop by the seat of government. Good-naturedly, he reimbursed Randall for the entire forty gallons when Randall returned in the spring of 1875.

That first winter of 1874-75, the most frequent volunteer carrier was the sheriff, John Greenell, who had come west three or four years earlier for his health. After he recovered, he easily became the most popular candidate of all in the election held the following summer. This is of little wonder, for not only did he bring mail to the snow-buried town, he also gave ski lessons to women and men alike.

The next winter he again began his legendary trips over Stony Pass. But one November day he didn't arrive at Silverton as scheduled. Searchers went out and eventually found the frozen man well off the usual trail. Possibly disoriented because of a head injury and suffering from hypothermia, he had laid down and frozen to death. The most popular man in the Animas country died doing for others what he liked doing best.

The snowbound communities were almost totally without communication to the outside world after December. Mule and burro trains stopped running over precarious Stony Pass, and it was necessary for those remaining – including several families – to largely exist upon supplies at hand. The little means of receiving and sending mail that existed was through volunteer carriers who made that treacherous seventy mile trip to Del Norte on "Norwegian snowshoes", as skis were then called.

As the populations of the remote mining camps grew and camps became towns, so did the demand for Uncle Sam to let out contracts to carry the mail. The payment to the men who carried the mail was not particularly high even in the furious winters if one bit of correspondence recounted in Frank Rice's manuscript on early Ouray is correct - and I'm sure it is:

In 1891 Washington wrote to Ouray postmaster Rice, seeking help in finding a reliable man to carry mail from Mineral Point to Animas Forks, Mineral Point to Ouray and Mineral Point to Silverton. The existing contract called for three trips a week at $4.00 per trip or more that $600 a year. Washington considered this exorbitant. The Washington connection felt $200 or even $250 each year would be ample payment, while recognizing that during winter months the carrier must travel on snowshoes through life endangering snowslides!

The legendary Otto Mears took the contract to supply Ouray's mail the first time the contract was offered. He soon found the men he hired for the job were unwilling to face the cold and dangers and soon quit. Mears procured sled dogs (heaven knows from where) and attempted to use them to pull a sled laden with mail; the dogs only floundered in the deep snow, and their use was impractical. Facing the possibility of some sort of legal action if he failed to carry out his contract, Mears strapped the heavy pouches on his own back and carried the mail all winter. He did not renew the contract for the following year.

Despite the dangerous work not paying very much, for some it was better than the alternative of sitting all winter in one of the San Juan communities without work, as most of the mines closed down. So men sought mail carrying contracts. Most carriers performed far above what local citizens would have expected. But there was the occasional rotten apple among the barrel of good ones. Such was the case of a man named McCann.

In 1879 a semi-weekly service was established between Silverton and San Miguel (the predecessor camp of Telluride). The carrier would leave Silverton and go up Mineral Creek to the trail heading over Ophir pass. Crossing the pass, he would then descend to Iron Springs, go on to Ophir (the little town we now call Old Ophir) and so on to present-day Society Turn where San Miguel was located. One day McCann did not turn up as scheduled. An investigation found his mail bag near Iron Springs cut open with a knife and the registered mail "rifled". According to the "*San Miguel Times*, McCann had left the country.

The usual mail carrier was totally honest and courageously met nature's challenges. "Scotty, the mail carrier from Ophir to Rico, nearly froze on his last trip," the *Ouray Times* recalled. In the winter of 1883 the route over Ophir Pass was reported by the same paper as perilous, with snowslides rampant. "Snow is four feet deep, and there are snowslides in every gulch . . ."

These were the conditions that mail carrier Swede Nilson faced as Christmas neared. He was warned he should not attempt his journey, but he brushed off the warnings because he didn't want to disappoint the excited and waiting families. He set off on December 23. He never arrived.

Search parties went out but could find no trace of the missing Nilson. When spring came again, a search was made but no trace of the missing carrier was found. Some people became convinced he had looted the mail and left the country. Finally in August of the next year, the melting snow of an avalanche revealed his body, the mail sack still strapped to him.

Mail was transported in a much less formal way in the 1800s. In this case a tree served as a post office. People going to town took mail and brought the incoming mail back.
— Author's collection

CHAPTER 16 🌵

A LAKE CALLED LENORE

A long time ago the First and Last Saloon of Ouray was located across from the Ouray Brickworks on the road to Montrose. The present swimming pool and hot springs is now located in the hole that once provided the bricks that were used to build many of Ouray's early structures, including the Beaumont Hotel. The saloon was owned by George Wettengel who also owned the Bon Ton dance hall on Second Street.

Wettengel had come to Ouray as a young man. He was a nephew of Gus Begole, who was the first to establish a mining claim in the valley. Gus found the rich Mineral Farm, the most successful of early Ouray mines. After he sold the mine, he established a grocery store on Main Street and employed two nephews. George Begole moved on from Ouray to Denver and became its mayor and was a highly respected citizen. George Wettengel took a completely opposite turn to became one of Ouray's undesired citizens.

The city fathers were inclined to close their eyes to the operations of the houses on Second Street as long as the proprietors paid their monthly "dues" to the city treasury and the "female boarding house" occupants paid their weekly fines. The parlor which Wettengel operated must have been particularly noxious, because the city fathers finally repealed Wettengel's license — an action very seldom taken. If Wettengel was to continue his profitable operation he would have to find a new location, somewhere outside Ouray.

Wettengel came up with the idea that as long as he had to move outside of the City of Ouray, why not establish a retreat in the country? So he leased land bordering a small lake called Manion's which was located alongside the Red Rock Canyon Road (now Dexter Creek) which went to the Calliope and Bachelor mines. There he built a roadhouse with a saloon and adequate rooms to house the customers overnight who he expected would come to patronize his girls.

Two of his girls, Julia and Lenore, were among the most popular of all the women in the "female boarding houses" of Ouray. With his new luxurious lakeside establishment and the star attraction of his two highly regarded girls, Wettengel was sure he had a winning combination.

Then came the question of a name for the little lake (much smaller than today since a dam has now been constructed enlarging the body of water). Naming the lake for one of his popular girls would help publicize his new establishment. He chose the name of the lovely dark-haired Lenore.

This choice immediately raised friction between his two headliners. Julia was jealous and hurt that her name was not selected, for until this point George had shown a distinct preference for her over the dark haired Lenore. Was George becoming fickle and about to set her aside for Lenore? George solved the potential conflict by marrying Julia.

The townspeople assumed that George had taken this way out to keep both of his attractive and in-demand girls. The new establishment opened with fanfare and for the first weeks did a booming business. But as the newness wore off, business fell. The major problem was the remoteness of the establishment. That four and a half mile walk on a cold winter night was very discouraging for the average miner who had to travel that distance on "shanks' mare," because he had no horse to ride. Despite the attractiveness of the girls, well there were other girls available right in town. And so the new establishment at Lake Lenore suffered and went out of business.

Sometime before the final closing of doors, Lenore saw the handwriting on the wall, or rather felt a decline of her earnings and left Ouray for another mining town where she would be in high demand. Of course Julia remained with George, since after all, they were married.

Then came the surprise to the townspeople. George gave up his former business and became a working citizen. And Julia became a housewife, but the two had no children. The years went by, and Julia became very ill. Wettengel became her personal nurse, caring for her until she died on September 9, 1928 at the age of fifty-nine. George Wettengel erected a fine granite headstone in her memory.

What followed made many a Ourayite ashamed of his lack of dedication to a passed loved one. For every day in the spring, summer, and autumn, George Wettengel walked the five miles each way to visit Julia's grave. Only in winter did he fail to make his daily visit, and then, according to old-timers, he trudged the five miles, back and forth, often through snow and mud at least three times a week. Finally one day in early October 1943, the day came when Wettengel could no longer walk that ten miles and Julia was left with the gold of the leaves of the surrounding trees to take the place of flowers. Wettengel died only a few days later on October 19, 1943. He lies beside his beloved Julia, but no stone has been placed to mark his resting place.

Perhaps the granite stone he erected to his beloved Julia is all the testimony of his life that is needed.

Lake Lenore is not only a beautiful spot but as shown in this 1902 photograph it was also filled with large and hungry rainbow trout. In the distance is Whitehouse Mountain.
— Courtesy of P. David Smith

CHAPTER 17

"FATHER, IT'S TIME TO PUT UP THE STOVE!"

Come October Mother was sure to comment on some chilly morning, "Father it's time to put up the stove!" Father would probably ignore the first comment, but eventually the horrendous task had to be faced.

During the summer we had gotten along very nicely with the kitchen stove and the small heater upstairs in our parents' bedroom. But now came the need for the big base burner.

The old stove had been stored away in the woodshed for the summer; now it must be dragged out. And this was a task not to be taken lightly — the stove was heavy indeed. The front of the stove was nickel work interspersed with isinglass windows. More nickel work decorated the corners and the top which had a knight, sword in hand, topping the whole.

To handle the task Father took half a day off from the Cascade Grocery, his partners filling in. First came the removal of the plate in the chimney that had closed the stove pipe hole all summer. With removal of the plate came a flood of soot, old leaves and perhaps a dead bird. All of this was the subject of a great flurry of cleaning supervised by Grandma LaRoche.

Next the stove pipes were brought forth, tapped on their ends to remove the old soot and given a blackening — all of this the task of us children and as result we were in need of cleaning too.

Then came the moving of the reluctant old stove up the back steps, through the doorway into the dining room. Inevitably doorways were scratched despite all the warnings by mother, and fingers were pinched and cut as well as backs strained.

In the dining room a six foot square of linoleum was laid and secured with strips of brass around the edges. Upon this was placed the zinc to insulate the floors against possible fire. The stove had to be lifted first over the linoleum and then over the zinc edge to arrive at its final setting.

The farther the stove was from the chimney hole, the longer the length of pipe required and the more heat through the room. All this provided the angle from the stove to the chimney was adequate to keep the stove from smoking. Somehow the lengths of pipe never properly fit the space to be covered, and the stove had to be moved another two inches or a length of pipe cut. Sometimes one length of pipe refused to fit inside another, and here too came comments upon the antecedents of stove and pipe manufacturers.

Eventually the task was finished, and supporting wires from the pipes were anchored to the ceiling. If enough supports were not secured, the pipe might fall during the winter and the resulting soot over household furnishings was beyond telling. The final task was telephoning Mr. Reynolds to hitch up his team and bring a load of lump coal to place in the shed. From the shed came the fuel which was carried in three or four coal buckets each morning and night — another chore for us children.

Sometimes I don't long for the "good old days."

This is the Henn family home in Ouray - the site of many tribulations as the father of the house struggled to get the pot bellied stove set up for winter. — AUTHOR'S FAMILY COLLECTION

CHAPTER 18

THE LOST SWEDE MINE

The first real snow of winter had fallen into the cliff-rimmed valley that held the little mining community of Ouray. Some six inches of wet soaking snow lay on the streets and building tops. Up in the mountains the six wet inches were replaced by two feet of cold powder snow that ninety years later would be avidly sought by skiers.

In those early days of big-time mining in the San Juans, the coming of winter meant one of two things: either the mining companies had earlier packed in food, clothing, and mining supplies sufficient to last the five or six months before spring so the mine could continue to operate or the mine was closed until the next spring, and the miners left to come down to the other towns of the San Juans. In those high regions where the mines were, the way was closed by what we now call avalanches. The old newspapers of those days are filled with stories of snowslides that tore apart mine buildings and killed workers. In some instances the damage was so extensive that all the surface workings were completely obliviated. Some of the loss of the extensive surface workings was so great the once productive mine was never reopened.

And so it was with this winter of eighty-five years ago. Many of the mines in the high country had closed for the winter. Miners from those mines had come down the long trails to Ouray and had sought boarding houses or their homes to spend the winter months.

Like other miners, the Swede had left the Golden Fleece, but instead of heading downward to Lake City as did most of his fellow miners (Lake City was only a few miles from the Golden Fleece) the Swede headed up the trail to Ouray. Four thousand feet higher and twelve miles later the Swede was crossing the American Flats headed for Ouray when the storm struck. The American Flats is a treeless expanse above timberline with very little shelter from a "blizzarding" storm. Struggling against the freezing winds and snows the Swede was hard pressed to cross the 12,000 foot flats and climb up and over 13,000 foot Engineer Pass and thus reach the Ouray-Uncompahgre watershed. The shortest way to get to Ouray was to find the gorge of

Bear Creek and follow Bear Creek Trail to its joining with the old Mears Toll Road that went from Red Mountain to Ouray. From the top of Engineer Pass down to the canyon trail there are at least three different routes that we have hiked, and there may well be more.

Seeking relief from the storm he plunged downward into one of the various gulches that eventually would lead to Bear Creek. Realizing the extreme danger he was in, the Swede unshouldered his pack and discarded it beside the trail. He stopped long enough to pull from the pack a couple of pairs of socks so he might put on warm and dry ones when he reached the shelter of the timber in the Bear Creek drainage and thus protect his feet from freezing in soaked shoes and socks.

The storm worsened, and the Swede could no longer see the trail. He feared a mis-step would plunge him over the cliff. So he turned away from the cliff side of the trail and sought shelter against the opposite side where the cliffs rose; virtually feeling his way, he found a crevasse he could squeeze into and which sheltered him from the bitter wind and the driving blizzard. Held upright in the narrow crack with protruding rocks digging into his back, the Swede was in a most unenviable position.

Uncomfortable as he was the Swede wiggled to relieve the pressure against his back. In doing so he became aware of a seam of quartz that ran perpendicular downward in front of him. To his amazement it was heavily laced with gold. Taking his knife he began to pry gold from the vein, and with a rock he pounded more ore loose. But what to carry the rocks of his find? His pack had been left miles above where he now was; the return to reach the pack through snow that by now was three feet deep was out of the question. The two pair of socks seemed the solution, and he filled them with his gold. This solution was to nearly be his undoing.

When the storm slackened he left his shelter and plunged downward on the trail. As the temperature fell his wet socks froze in his soaked shoes, and six miles later when he reached the outskirts of Ouray he was suffering from frost bite and so numb he stumbled as he walked. When he stumbled into the Gold Belt Dance Hall and Saloon, it was obvious to both the customers and the dance hall girls that he needed immediate assistance. The ice clinging to his eyelashes, face and clothing obscured his features, and at first he was unrecognizable.

His frozen shoes were pulled from his feet and a bucket of snow brought from outside to rub them. His frozen jacket was peeled from him, and underneath was revealed the four socks filled with rich highgrade. When this was found, work on the nearly frozen Swede was suspended while all - miners, girls, and barkeeper — examined his wondrous haul. Then he was plied with whiskey, his hands, feet, and body massaged in hopes he would soon tell of how he came upon the socks full of highgrade ore.

With reluctance he told his story — he could do little else under the circumstances — and the highgrade was taken to the saloon safe to be locked up until the morrow. Quite a "discussion" arose among the girls as to which one would take him to her bed to see that he was adequately warmed. . . . a new experience for the Swede who had never before found himself the object of attention from several ladies.

As it turned out the next day, after the ore had been assayed, it was indeed a very rich find. And the Swede had sufficient money to live comfortably with female companionship all the winter. In fact the produce was sufficient that it was unnecessary for the Swede to return to mining or prospecting the next summer, or for that matter, for the following winter.

But in the second summer the girls in the "female boarding houses" (as defined by the United States Census) had turned from Swede. His money had been spent. So he set forth to relocate his mine.

When he climbed to the upper reaches of the Bear Creek drainage he was confused. Nothing looked the same as it had in the blizzard. In fact he was even uncertain as to which of the various gulch trails he had followed down to Bear Creek. He searched and he searched, but he never found that crevasse he had crawled into during the height of the blizzard.

Experienced hikers in the Rockies are well aware that landmarks are easily lost, even by simply looking for them when going the opposite direction. The San Juan Mountains are the subject of frequent snowslides, and these avalanches could well have buried the crevasse under tons of rock.

The Swede searched and searched for many summers. The frustration and the laughs of those who poked fun at his efforts resulted in his slowly going mad. He was carried to the Pueblo Asylum where he died.

One would think the story of the Lost Swede Mine would end there. But it didn't. Some quarter of a century later a telephone crew was working on the old telephone line that ran from Ouray up Bear Creek Canyon to Poughkeepsie Gulch and over the American Flats to Lake City. The young men working on this project would often go hiking and exploring in the evening after their work was done. On one such occasion one of them saw an unusual rock lying along the route he was scrambling, and because it was unusual he dropped the ore in his pocket. Two years later he happened to show it to an old-timer who immediately identified it as the same ore found by the Swede. But according to the finder, it was simply lying on the ground, probably "float" that is, ore that had broken loose from its origin and rolled to where it was found.

If searchers could start from where the "float" was found, they very likely would be able to trace its path to its point of origin; that is the way many mines have been found. Unfortunately the young man who had found the "float" had absolutely no remembrance of where he found it.

And so the "Lost Swede Mine" still remains lost. Will you find it? Will it ever be found?

(This story is told the way it was related to me by the men down at Johnny Donald's Livery stable. They told wondrous stories with wondrous words. One old burro puncher couldn't speak five words without interjecting a swear word. He was the one who told me this story. I wish I could retell it in the picturesque language he used; if I did it would never be printed. But those tough old-timers were ever so kind to a fatherless boy. I remember them with deep appreciation.)

This photograph of American Flats shows the incredible ruggedness of the area. No wonder the Swede couldn't find his way back to his valuable discovery.
— BILL FRIES PHOTO,
COURTESY OF P. DAVID SMITH

CHAPTER 19

THE TRIP TO ORGANIZE THE OURAY CHURCH - 1877

After a pleasant Sabbath spent at the little church at Lake City and then with Rev. Darley and his family, we started early one Monday morning to Ouray. Taking the stage to Capitol City, we traveled up the canyon of Hermosa Creek for ten miles, passing between lofty rock walls from 100 to 1,000 feet high. By noon we were at Capitol. After a good lunch we shouldered our blankets and provisions and started on foot up the canyon. All along are beautiful waterfalls and cascades a thousand feet high. Here and there we passed areas where avalanches had cut a broad swath down the mountainside, carrying away trees, and leaving but stumps and limbs. Five miles up at the edge of the snow line, we come to a new log cabin built by Messers. Smith and Harris. Here we camped for the night. We knew that it would freeze hard during the night allowing us to cross on the crust of the snow, but not otherwise.

About sundown the clouds began to gather and snow to fall and with it our hopes of crossing the pass. But earnest prayer was made that He who causes the elements to do His bidding would so control them that we could get across, but not otherwise.

Our blankets were spread upon a pile of shingles, and I was soon sleeping soundly. Mr. Darley, who could not sleep, kept the fire burning and amused himself by throwing chips of wood at the chipmunks that played about the floor and ran over our beds. About 2 a.m. he announced that breakfast was ready. Eating a breakfast of bacon, biscuits and coffee by half past three, we were on our way to get over the crest before the morning sun should soften it.

We traveled over fallen timber in the dark, felt our way across logs that spanned streams, or waded the creeks, and when boots and socks were thoroughly wet we found grim satisfaction in wading all subsequent streams rather than balancing on an uncertain log. In an hour we were at timberline — the elevation where timber ceases to grow. We now started zigzagging up the vast field of frozen snow and ice. The air grew rarer and rarer and breathing became more and

This photograph appears in Rev. Darley's book *Pioneering in the San Juans* and shows him (right) and another traveler on skis just outside Ouray. — AUTHOR'S COLLECTION

more difficult. The wet boots became frozen too. Still up and up we went. With each step the heel of the boot would be driven firmly into the frozen snow — each one trying to step in the dent made by the one preceding him. A misstep would send the unlucky traveler sliding down the snow face of the mountain to be dashed to pieces on the rocks below. Every few steps, securing our heels in the snow, we would lay out full length exhausted, hearts' thumping, noses' bleeding, eyes' running and ears' ringing. Sometimes the blood is forced from both eyes and ears. From near the summit a detached rock was sent whirling down the vast snowfield, until a mile below it seemed like a top spinning on the floor.

Daylight was approaching, and still we were painfully climbing when, as the first rays of morning sun were lighting up a hundred grand peaks around, we gained the summit of 13,000 feet. And from the summit, what a panorama greeted our eyes. . . .

But it was too cold to tarry, and we were soon plunging down the western face of the mountains. When it was not too deep we could run down the face of the snow, and where it was too deep for running, we could sit down and slide. And such a slide of a thousand feet, at breakneck speed, would be a great event for the average schoolboy.

Between running and sliding we were down in twenty minutes, a distance that on the other side had taken two hours of painful climbing, and were at the first cabin at the head waters of the Uncompahgre River. Without halting we plunged down the canyon as there was still considerable snow to be crossed. Soon after reaching timberline the snow ran out and we met a succession of dry ground and mud. Down we went until we reached Poughkeepsie Creek, which through a wild and almost inaccessible canyon joins the Uncompahgre from the west.

Here we lost the trail and got off into fallen timber. By the time the trail was found, my feet were so blistered from traveling in wet and at times frozen boots, that I could go no further. We were in the heart of the mountains still ten miles from town. It was decided Mr. Darley should leave the provisions and blankets with me and push on to Ouray and send back a horse to carry me in. Building a fire I went to sleep with my feet drying at the fire.

Four hours passed and Mr. Darley returned without the horse. Shortly after leaving me, he had gotten lost, and wandered around until he found himself in the bottom of a deep canyon, where the water of the mountain torrent shut off all further progress. To extricate himself from that gorge he had climbed great pine trees, that like stairs enabled him to get from one ledge to another. On his return he met a miner going to Ouray and being too exhausted to walk with him, had sent a note informing the Presbyterians of our situation.

After a good rest, a burro pack train came along, and we hired our passage into Ouray on the same kind of animal on which our Savior made his triumphant entry into Jerusalem. So mounting a burro without saddle or bridle we started for town.

— SHELDON JACKSON

CHAPTER 20

UNCLE DICK WOOTON AND HIS SHEEP

"Uncle Dick" Wooton came to the Rockies in 1836 at age twenty. His life is one of the better chronicled of the mountain men, having recounted his life and adventures to a reputable writer before he died in 1893. The account of his adventures can be cross checked against other known reported facts.

In his travels he criss-crossed all of the West to the California Spanish settlements and from Oregon down into Mexico. When the California gold rush began he strongly recommended use of the Old Spanish Trail. The trail was never a single strand but had a multiplicity of branches, all eventually going the same way from the New Mexico Spanish settlements to the California ones.

Uncle Dick's preference was from Santa Fe up the Rio Grande River, crossing the Continental Divide at Cochetopa Pass, following down and crossing mountains to the Uncompahgre (much of the time generally following the present route of Highway 50 to the present site of Montrose). From here it was along the Uncompahgre until the Gunnison was reached, then down to the Grand (now Colorado) River where it crossed into Utah and hence by alternating routes all the way to the California Coast.

In 1852 he pioneered a new adventure that was followed in subsequent years by several others. He gathered a herd of 9,000 sheep from near Watrous, New Mexico, and carefully lashing supplies on a string of mules, set forth for California. Included in the pack train's supplies were $1,000 worth of flour, sugar, dried meat and ammunition. He employed fourteen New Mexican sheepherders and eight guards. The guards were either former soldiers or teamsters but turned out to be so inexperienced in mountain warfare, that "Uncle Dick" had to rely entirely on his own resources. To aid the Mexican herders, eight goats were used, two leading the way each day and the other six engaged in herding. A single dog closed up the stragglers into the main herd. And thus they journeyed from Taos toward the Sacramento Valley.

Just short of the source of the Rio Grande, the party turned north over the Continental Divide and Cochetopa Pass. At Eagle Tail River, west of Cochetopa Pass, the expedition was confronted by a band of Utes. The Indians tried to scatter the flock by rifle shots, but this only drove the sheep nearer to the herders for protection. Chief Uncotash finally rode into "Uncle Dick's" camp demanding a tribute for the sheep crossing the Ute's lands. With his guards being of little use, Wooton took the initiative and grappled with the Indian and pinned him to the ground. By placing his wicked looking knife across the Indian's throat, "Uncle Dick" negotiated and secured a compromise and gave to the Indians some flour and ammunition. Uncotash's warriors stood by, helpless to intervene for fear the knife would slash their Chief's throat.

Reaching the Uncompahgre, Wooton drove them up a way to excellent pasture he knew of and rested the flock before heading onward. Could this have been what we call "Cow Creek" today? One wonders how Wooton knew of the lush pastures if he had not traveled up the Uncompahgre in years past during his extensive wanderings. Had he passed through the future site of Ouray? Entirely possible.

During his trip the first domestic herds of sheep had been pastured in the San Juans which was to know the sharp hooves of later flocks of sheep which have and still graze on our high mountain grasslands.

Sheep now cover the San Juan high country. In this photograph they are being dipped for parasites before they make their journey to the mountains.
— COURTESY OF P. DAVID SMITH

CHAPTER 21 🌿

BURROS, JACKASSES BUT NEVER DONKEYS

It was in Sunday school that I first heard the word donkey. It must have been a Palm Sunday lesson, because the lesson included reference to an "ass." None of my five-year-old classmates were any better informed than I was and one of us demanded to know what an ass was. "Why," the teacher answered "An ass is a donkey!" We all looked at her in confusion, "But what is a donkey?"

Our teacher must have been one of those public school teachers, imported from the outside world, because she had little understanding of the world which we, born in Ouray, knew. "Why there are donkeys all around Ouray;" and then seeing our still confused faces she added, "You know, they are like a horse, except they are smaller and have long ears."

Now, we came to understanding, "You mean burros — and burros are donkeys and donkeys are asses!" But we all thought, "Why would anyone want to call a burro an ass or a donkey?"

Burros thoroughly occupied Ouray. They were picketed in almost every vacant lot; the corrals at the stables were filled with them, and housewives were hard put to keep loose burros from eating the flowers and vegetables in the gardens.

It hardly seems possible that the San Juans could have been settled without the burro. In the very early years the trails into Silverton, Ouray, Telluride and Lake City were too narrow and rough to accommodate teams of oxen. Indeed getting into any of the local towns in a wagon pulled by any kind of animal was a very difficult problem to solve. Pack trains were the major source of transportation into the mountains, and there were many more burros used than mules.

The term "pack train" really doesn't fit in dealing with burros. You could successfully lead horses or mules, but the horses could not carry the loads day after day that the mule could. Burros cannot be successfully led, rather they are driven and lead the way up and down the narrow trails on the mountainsides. Attempting to lead burros was out of the question.

Burros could not carry the same size load as mules, but mules had to be fed and cared for. Burros were simply turned loose to find their own food. It used to be said that burros would even eat cans; more likely they were rummaging in the cans for any leftovers, but they did enjoy eating the paper labels off the cans.

Burros brought the first loads of supplies into the San Juans. The first minister to arrive in Ouray (Rev. George Darley) came from Lake City via the Gunnison and Uncompahgre Rivers in a frightful snowstorm. While following the Uncompahgre they needed to cross back and forth over its cold, rushing waters — fourteen times in sixteen miles. The burro that carried their packs, after a couple of crossings, stood firm in his determination that enough was enough. It was necessary for the two travelers to seize the animal by the head and tail and throw him into the river at each of the following twelve crossings. Bitter and cold though it was, the burro did get their packs safely to Ouray. This I can not vouch for, but it was told that to get a burro successfully across a deep stream, it was necessary to tie his ears up, because if water were to get in its ears, he would drown.

Nearly every boy in Ouray had his own burro since they were cheap — even free — and their care cost little. Burros lived a surprisingly long life. Queenie, one of our family's pets, at the age of twenty eight had a strong and healthy colt. She was still very much alive when we left Ouray for Denver, so how old she lived to be, I have no idea.

Dad had the theory that every child should have animals to care for, and hence all of us had a burro as our personal responsibility. . . to feed, to curry, and to ride. That small herd left Father with the problem of where to keep them during the winter months when they couldn't be ridden and feeding was expensive. (It was unthinkable that our burros should be left to fend for themselves.)

One winter Father came up with a great idea. During the previous summer a hard-working young Italian couple had moved onto a small tract of land just down the valley where they "truck gardened". The produce they raised was high quality, so Father (one of the partners in the Cascade Grocery) stocked a great deal of their vegetables that summer. But he had a concern as to how the young couple would survive during the winter when truck gardening was out. It hit him that he would send our burros down to the truck farm and let

This prospector has loaded up his faithful burros and is headed off into the hills with enough equipment and supplies to sustain him and his animals for months.

— AUTHOR'S COLLECTION

them graze and be fed by the young couple. As it turned out Father needn't have been concerned about them, for the couple knew how to take care of themselves. They soon turned up at the Cascade selling delicious salami. It was so good that our family ate a great deal of that flavorful salami that winter. Father never thought to question where the meat came from that was ground up and pressed into salami rolls. The next spring we found out. Not a single one of our burros had survived; they had all gone through the grinder to make the delicious salami we had enjoyed.

In some ways those burros raised us. For example, if we mistreated Queenie when trying to get her to go faster than she thought she should go, she would simply flop down on the ground, capturing at least one of our legs underneath her. Yelling and hitting her did no good, neither did crying, a leg underneath a burro, probably resting on a protruding rock, did hurt. When Queenie was sure we had been punished enough, she would rise with dignity, permit us to get in the saddle and would placidly go on her way, which we would hope would be the same way that we wanted to go.

Saddling a burro was a contest of wills between boy and burro. Throwing the burro saddle on its back was the simple part. The problem was getting the cinch tight enough so the saddle would remain upright and not slide around under the belly. The burro knew enough to take a deep breath and swell itself just as you would pull on the cinch. The burro would wait a moment until your attention was elsewhere and then relax and the cinch would be dangerously loose, forecasting a tumble at some point in your ride when the saddle started slipping. Out-waiting and out-witting the burro was a challenge.

If you did succeed in getting the cinch tightened properly, watch out! For very likely said burro would step on your foot, crushing it against the ground and refusing to move no matter how you kicked, hit or stormed.

All we youngsters became connoisseurs of burros at a very early age. I must have been about three when Father rented a buggy drawn by two horses (one with a colt that trotted alongside) and our family of six drove down the valley and up to a mountain ranch to spend the day. There are two outstanding memories of that trip. The first was going to the barn and climbing into the hayloft to find that the hayloft also had a ground level entrance (it was built on a hillside). The other memory was of passing a burro by the side of the road with a foal nursing; what made it memorable was that the colt was pure white without blemish of color. It was the only pure white burro I ever remember seeing — usually burros were gray or else a muddy brown, usually with a slash or two of white.

For boys who were burro owners, the Fourth of July celebration was most important. Every boy entered his burro into the burro race; indeed the number was so great two or three races had to be held. All games and activities centered around Main Street and were held in the block occupied by the Post Office Store (now it is the V & S Variety) and the Cascade Grocery (now Pricco's). One never knew what a burro would do amid the shouting noisy crowd; the results were often hilarious — that is, to everyone but the boy who found himself on a burro running the wrong direction or bucked off and laying flat in the dust of the unpaved street.

That brings up the other burro contest - the Burro Bucking Contest. That offered a problem, for every effort was usually expended to make the burros, gentle and free of bucking. So they had to be retrained to buck. One solution was to teach them to buck when bareback, but not when saddled. For some it meant having to walk, leading the burro if it had been out grazing some distance away;

otherwise trying to ride bareback would mean being thrown. I well remember going with my brother to fetch Queenie from where she had been grazing and brother Frank putting me up on her back to ride home while he led her. That summer he had been working unsuccessfully to train her for bucking in the Fourth of July contest. As he had been unsuccessful, Frank thought it safe to have me ride. We came down the hill successfully toward our home until we reached a hillside where ashes and cinder had been dumped for many years. There Queenie set her fore feet and pitched me right down that hillside of cinders. I was a thoroughly scratched and bleeding little boy who ran home to have Grandma apply soap and iodine. Burros never did the expected.

During the summer we would take the burros out to a nearby mountain meadow and turn them loose to graze, strapping a "burro bell" around their necks (I still have one of the burro bells in my possession). But when morning came, trying to find the burros was often a major problem. They would hide in a thicket of aspen trees and stand absolutely still so the bell around their necks would not ring.

Around our home, "burro" was the word used. Around the corrals and barns, which fascinated a boy and provided a liberal education, it was "jackass." We boys early learned to differentiate which word to use at which location; Grandmother's switch was a quick teacher. But use donkey? Never!!

CHAPTER 22

CAPITOL CITY

I first learned of Capitol City when I looked down on it from high above when we were sampling the dump at the Ocean Wave Mine. That was in the mid-1930s, but it was almost thirty years later before I was able to set foot in the old mining camp. Looking down from the Ocean Wave dump (and I often wondered how it got that fanciful name so many thousands of miles from an ocean) we could see a large brick house, which from that distance looked to be in reasonably good condition. There were a number of frame cabins, more or less derelict, and a large frame building at the opposite end of the park from the brick one. It seems to me that we left the Henson Creek road, perhaps a mile above Capitol City at the remains of some sort of a mill. From the mill site a trail left to climb to the Ocean Wave. Henson Creek runs from the base of Engineer Mountain downward to Lake City where it joins the Lake Fork of the Gunnison.

As I mentioned, it was thirty years later before I set foot in the old mining camp site. As had happened in most of the San Juans during World War II the opportunity to collect and sell metal for salvage had resulted in decimation of the old buildings and mills along Henson Creek. There were no buildings left at the Ocean Wave. All that remained of the brick home that might have been built as a future residence of Colorado's governors was a falling down wall. The large frame buildings at the opposite end of the park were gone and so was almost all evidence of log cabins.

The very name, Capitol City, suggests the confusion that surrounds this "city" on the Lake City-Engineer Pass road. Surely it should not be spelled with an "a" as in "Capital City," the way the revisionists of San Juan history insist on spelling it. But they know little of the peculiarities of the past in our San Juans.

The correct spelling is with an "o" as designated by George T. Lee who poured money into the Capitol City area and even took money out. The camp had been called Galena City until Lee took over. It is said Lee had dreams of the camp becoming the capitol of

This early day photograph shows Lake City in 1877. It was just a few years after the city was founded but it is already very well developed. — AUTHOR'S COLLECTION

Colorado, hence he changed the name to "Capitol" a spelling that indicates a building, such as the United States Capitol in Washington. Lee had big plans, and indeed he accomplished much in the 1870s and early 1880s. He built a smelting works a short distance below Capitol City, and also had a sawmill from which he delivered lumber and shingles to Lake City and mines as far away as Mineral Point. He had in use a hundred burro pack train for deliveries. A depression in the early 1880s in the Lake City area brought about by a lack of rail transport which was nearly the end of Capitol City. Then came the collapse of silver prices in 1893, which devastated mining in all of the San Juans. However gold was found in the old workings which had been originally devoted to mining silver.

Reportedly 700 people lived in the camp during the '90s when gold was being produced.

The camp had many frame houses, stores, a post office, saloons and the big frame building I saw many years ago which was the school, which tradition says was even designed by an architect hired by Lee. Lee also operated a marble quarry, a brick factory and a smelter. A second smelter also operated just above Capitol City. It must have been the smelter's ruin, which I mistook for a mill those many years when we took off to climb to the Ocean Wave. Incidentally, the Ocean Wave was reportedly shut down because of family discord and not because of lack of ore - - that was the reason we were sampling the dump to see if there was sufficient evidence to cause us to pay several years of back taxes and gain possession.

One evidence of George Lee's dynamic presence is still standing; that is a lime kiln he operated around 1880. The kiln has now been accepted and is a part of the National Register of Historic Places. The Ocean Wave was not a significant producer in the early Lake City area as was the Ute-Ulay or Golden Fleece. Located in 1876, the finders of the Ocean Wave promptly sold it to Kansas City capitalists who determined to construct a smelter to handle its difficult ores.

The Lake City fathers were delighted to support this endeavor which would supplement the already existing Crook's Concentration Works. They donated five complete city blocks to the Ocean Wave for construction of the smelter which went into operation the last of 1878. In recent years Lake City has renamed a street Ocean Wave Drive, more in memory of the smelter which was salvaged for metal about the time of World War II than for the mine.

Capitol City was a "Boom or Bust" camp. It prospered in the Seventies, crashed in the Eighties and boomed again in the Nineties. Again during this century it was up and down, although it never reached the population of the Nineties when gold production was great. As late as 1914 the post office was still open. Today, it is difficult to picture the once bustling camp with children riding burros, wash hanging from clotheslines and the incessant pounding of the stamps as mills pulverized rock from the mines to separate out the gold.

CHAPTER 23 🌿

GHOST STORIES —
THE GHOST WHO WALKS IN THE MUSEUM

The old hospital served Ouray and the surrounding communities for many, many years. It was originally built from contributions from miners, mine owners, and townsfolk. A sturdy stone and brick building, it continues to serve as the home of the Ouray County Historical Society.

The conversion from an abandoned hospital to a museum did not come easily. Hundreds and hundreds of volunteer hours were involved. Each progressive improvement required great faith and effort. Each administration has succeeded in making improvements, although funds have been scarce. When attorney P. David Smith was president of the museum, his big effort was to renovate the basement into a mine. Several board members also contributed their time to see this dream accomplished.

Smith was working in the evening in the basement putting rough boards in the wall to simulate the interior of buildings at the entrance of a mine tunnel. He was working at a time the museum was not open to the public, so they kept the door locked. One night he was in the basement of the museum and heard the sound of footsteps overhead. The steps could be heard from the front door going toward the back of the hall where the stairway to the basement went down.

He froze and listened to the approaching sound of the steps which proceeded to the head of the stairs, and then there was silence. Perhaps a single minute passed into what seemed like an hour. Was the unknown person waiting at the head of the stairs for him to come up? There was no other exit from the basement. He must go up those stairs and face whatever awaited him. He tip-toed up the steps to the first floor, but there was absolutely no one there. That's how I first heard of the Museum's ghost.

If there are ghosts, what better location to find them than in an old hospital. But are there ghosts? I didn't believe that there were. Then I had my experience.

About three years later, the museum board raised sufficient money to fire up the old coal furnace. Keeping the hospital at a constant temperature would better preserve the exhibits. This also made it practical to keep a half-time curator year around, for now he had a warm place he could work on collections. Part of the new curator's job description called for him to fire the old coal furnace. This was a dirty job, as it was in a sub-basement down another flight of steps from the basement we were using as the mining exhibition — the same basement that David had been transforming into the mine three years earlier when he had his encounter with the museum ghost. This sub-basement was very nasty, everything covered with coal dust, and the floor often ankle deep in water from the warm water spring that seeped through the walls.

Then our part-time curator broke his leg. The museum society had insufficient funds to keep him on the payroll and pay for someone to take care of the furnace - removing clinkers and feeding the beast coal in the morning. To have a fire to feed in the morning also meant a late afternoon trip to feed the furnace a second time, otherwise it went out and had to be rekindled. As president of the society that particular year, the task of working on the furnace twice a day fell on me.

How I hated that requirement. It meant putting on old clothes early every morning and going to the museum where I descended downward two flights of stairs in virtual darkness. At the bottom, I waded through groundwater that covered the floor to fill up buckets of coal; and I waded through the water again to empty the buckets into the hopper of the stoker; finally I waded to the stairs and began the climb up two floors to light and what seemed like freedom. To do this twice a day, as an unpaid volunteer!

In taking care of the furnace I always made sure I did so during daylight for the ease of walking through dark hallways and darker stairs. Then came the afternoon I didn't get the furnace fed on schedule. Trying to rebuild the fire after it went out was such a task that although it was dark, down to the museum I hiked, unlocked the door and using a flashlight proceeded down the long hall and down the steps to the basement.

The Sisters of Mercy built Ouray's first hospital and operated it for many years. Many a poor miner died here after a horrible accident. What better place to find a ghost!
— Courtesy of P. David Smith

I had turned at the landing and started down the next portion of the flight going to the exhibition basement when I heard the sound of footsteps walking down the hall I had just come from. I stopped. I knew the outside door had an automatic lock that would spring in place when I closed the door, so I couldn't imagine how anyone could have entered. I turned around and went back up the stairs and peered down the long hall; the hall did have a twist in it, but as far as I could see there was no one there. "It must have been my imagination," I thought. I started down the steps, and when I reached the landing I thought I heard those footsteps again. By the time I reached the basement floor I was sure whoever, or whatever, was standing at the head of the stairs.

Somewhat shakily I started down the stairs leading to the sub-basement. When I reached the landing on the first flight I could hear the footsteps descending to the landing on the first flight. "Well," I thought. "It can't get much worse than this," and I headed down the final steps to the nasty, wet furnace room floor.

But it did get worse. As I waded through the water, I could hear the footsteps coming on down the stairs to the furnace room, and I knew who, or whatever, was standing on that landing looking downward to where I labored. I turned my flashlight up to the landing, but could see nothing but blackness. I finished my job of shoveling coal into the buckets, wading with them to the hopper, and dumping them. I might add, looking over my shoulder the whole time.

Then I was faced with an awful decision. There was no way out of that hole except up the stairs, and I would walk right into what was waiting for me. The alternative was spending a night in that awful wet hole. There really wasn't a choice. Now I appreciated what Smith had gone through three years earlier. I started up those stairs, and while I didn't have a heart attack, I certainly knew what people meant when they said they had their hearts in their throats. Up I went, nothing on the landing; up again and nothing on the mining exhibition floor. Although I beamed my light here and there from the stairs, I didn't go looking behind doorways! Up again I climbed until I finally reached the first floor to run down the long corridor and escape outside.

There have been others who experienced the museum ghost. One of these was the half-time curator who worked the other half day for Ouray Social Services. He often dealt with family problems and was called out late at night. As he lived down the valley in Ridgway, sometimes after a late night call he would go to the museum, crawl onto a museum hospital bed and sleep rather than making a long ride home. Several times he was aware of the ghost coming to look in on him. He felt it was a curious ghost, not one that meant evil, and I guess he is right.

I still don't believe in ghosts - or do I? Never have I gone back alone at night into a museum that was once a hospital!

CHAPTER 24

GHOST STORIES — THE CEMETERY GHOST CAT

In the very early years traveling from Montrose south toward Ouray was very difficult. It was impossible to follow the banks of the Uncompahgre River, because it cut through several very narrow defiles which offered no space between river bed and cliff. To get around these obstacles the pioneers left the Uncompahgre near the Indian Agency which was located at present-day Colona. From Colona they made a rough road which is now the major county road access to Log Hill coming from the north. When they arrived at the southern edge of Log Hill they faced the daunting problem of lowering wagons from the top of the mesa to the level of the creek bed below. As was commonly done on steep descents, whether it was a four-horse team or one of several yokes of oxen, most of the animals would be unhitched from the front and instead hitched to the rear to help hold back the wagon from rushing "helter-skelter" to the bottom. This system of braking was still sometimes inadequate, in which case ropes were secured to the wagon and looped around trees and with a man or two on the end of each rope the wagon could be lowered by degrees.

Obviously by the time the wagon was lowered to the banks of Dallas Creek, the animals and men were exhausted. If they arrived late in the day a camp would be made. An alternative to making camp and cooking dinner on a campfire was provided by an elderly couple who had built a relatively small cabin nearby. They would often permit travelers to bed down in front of their fireplace and enjoy a dinner they had prepared. The couple was obviously quite popular among the travelers who made the difficult journey.

A number of years ago I served as president of the Ouray Cemetery District and became friendly with the old gentleman who had served for many years as caretaker of Cedar Hill Cemetery. It wasn't easy to communicate with him because of his extreme deafness, but he was a wonderful person and the cemetery was well served by his employment. He told me many stories of those who lay asleep in the lovely sloping grounds of Cedar Hill.

No one has ever gotten a photograph of the ghost cat but the author thought this photograph of a two-holer outhouse was just as interesting. There is a tall one for adults and a small one for children. — AUTHOR'S PHOTO

One day he asked me if I'd seen the cat. "What cat?" I asked. "Why," he replied, "the ghost cat that lives in the cemetery."

When I showed my skepticism he told me to go up and across the upper irrigation ditch, not far from a great willow, and perhaps I would see the cat. I hiked to where he told me to look, but I didn't see any cat.

Many mornings when I stopped to talk with him, he would tell me he'd seen the cat, why didn't I go and look. I would; but I never saw the cat. Finally he told me the story of the ghost cat.

That older couple that lived on the banks of Dallas Creek had a lovely big white cat, which purringly welcomed travelers to the couples' home. One night as they were banking the fire in preparation for bedtime, a stranger knocked on the door and asked to be put up for the night. Despite being ready to go to bed, they asked him to come in, warmed up the left-overs from their evening supper and fed him. He wasn't a person who appealed to either of them, but they permitted him to take a blanket and lie down in front of the fire. The strangest thing was the actions of the cat. Instead of purring a welcome when the stranger entered, the cat arched his back and spit. The cat was so nasty that one of the couple finally put him outside for the night.

The next morning passers-bys did not notice either of the old couple outside or smoke coming from the chimney. That wasn't necessarily unusual, so no one immediately investigated. It wasn't until evening that a teamster, who had just come down from Log Hill, went to the cabin to see if he could spent the night. Outside the door he found the cat with its head smashed. When he opened the door he found both the man and the woman lying in pools of dried blood. The killer was never found, and the murders remain unsolved.

The bodies were carried to Cedar Hill Cemetery and buried. But the strange thing was, that the morning after the burial, a passer-by reported seeing a white cat sitting on the mounds of the new graves. Although it has been seen many times by others, I never saw the ghost white cat. New officers of the cemetery district have secured a family to live on the grounds, and they are far better cared for than before. Newspaper reports are that the groundkeepers have also seen the ghost white cat!

CHAPTER 25

THE UNCOMPAHGRE RIVER, BEAR CREEK FALLS AND INDIAN TEARS

The Uncompahgre River is a mess! Ugly and reddish orange, it is anything but the clear rushing stream that we picture in our minds as coming from melting mountain snow. When a boy in the Ouray schools, we were taught that Uncompahgre meant "Father of Hot Waters." That made sense, because in the bed of the stream are numerous hot springs, and from early accounts, many, many hot springs at one time gurgled forth in the basin that is now the city of Ouray.

The journals of the Fathers Escalante and Dominques record quite a different story as to the meaning. It seems that when the wandering fathers came off the mesa and down into the Uncompahgre Valley, they asked their Indian guide, "What river is this?" He replied with guttural grunts which we translate today as "Uncompahgre." Asked by the fathers what that meant, he indicated that it meant the river was dirty and nasty - or words to that effect. Even then, in 1776, the Uncompahgre was a highly polluted river.

Further the river is a mess because it doesn't originate where it logically should. Obviously it should follow the deepest canyon which would lead up to the top of Red Mountain Pass. But it doesn't. Instead it turns away from the deep canyon and follows a tributary up the gorge that we now know as the Engineer Mountain-Lake City route. From the lower end of that gorge it dashes in a great fall down the canyon into what is Red Mountain Creek at a place all old-timers called "State Bridge," named because the state furnished the money to build the cement bridge across what was then a chasm (sometime in more recent years, the chasm had been filled in and the Uncompahgre channeled to run down the fill in rapids rather than a fall). At that point the Uncompahgre was a clear rushing torrent; it was when it joined Red Mountain Creek (flowing from the three Red Mountains) that it became "dirty and nasty".

Why is it that this tributary to what is obviously the main canyon is named the Uncompahgre while the river following down the deep canyon is called Red Mountain Creek?

The answer comes from the route that early discoverers took to reach the valley in which now is located the City of Ouray. Mineral Point, at the foot of Engineer Mountain and also at the head of the Animas River, was a booming mining camp in 1875, the first claims in the area having been filed in 1873.

From the mining camp of Mineral Point the prospectors followed the stream (now called Uncompahgre) to finally reach the site of the future Ouray. The course they followed was designated the Uncompahgre River. It doesn't make much sense, but then the Uncompahgre has never been a very logical river.

About four miles south of Ouray, along the Million Dollar Highway, is Bear Creek Falls. At one time there was a sign placed there that told the story of the falls, the toll house which once stood there and some information about Otto Mears. The highway department viewed the sign as a hazard and removed it, fearing too many tourists might stop to read the sign, look at the spectacular falls, and thus impede traffic. Well many tourists still stop to look, and now they know nothing about what they see!

And spectacular it is! Bear Creek rushing down the mountainside in a series of falls and rapids; passes under a bridge at the Million Dollar Highway, shoots outward into the Uncompahgre Canyon, and falls more than 200 feet to the river below. It was at this crossing of the falls that the ingenious Otto Mears placed his tollhouse, thus assuring that all who traveled the canyon would have to pay before proceeding.

Even before Otto Mears built a substantial bridge and his tollhouse, the crossing was notorious to travelers, both miners and tourists. Here is the record of an early congressman traveling from Lake City to Ouray:

"As they descended to the point of the great hill, shaped like the hump on a camel, there swept before them Bear Creek Falls, the greatest combination of wild yawning chasms, mighty towering cliffs, merciless, grinding roaring waters, with gentle, misty sprays, great chaste, white spreading bridal veils, variegated rainbows, and symmetrical white stray domes, crouched, ghost-like, on the smooth cliffs below, that has been discovered on this continent, if not in the world . . . ."

"The bed of the Uncompahgre River here is cut many, many hundred feet down into these majestic cliffs, and the trail in the cliff around an obtuse angle between Bear Creek and the Uncompahgre River is gouged out of solid rock for quite a distance, just wide enough for a horse to go around . . . it is many hundred feet from trail to the top of the cliffs and even further from the trail to the bed of the river below."

" A crude bridge, consisting of three logs side by side with a few chips and a little dirt thrown onto the creases between them, laid across the narrow stone box channel of Bear Creek where it dumps its raging waters over high cliffs, constitutes the only possible crossing. ...for getting into Ouray .... The mining superintendent, with his head skyward, rode his horse over the frail structure."

"Mr. Whickham dismounted, tied up his bridle, went back, got a firm hold on the large part of his horse's tail, fixed his eyes above the hips of his horse and followed him over. The mining expert tied up his bridle, stepped behind his horse, gave him a lash with his rawhide, and the horse walked over; the expert got down on his stomach, turned his head up like a fur seal, when about to be fed, and crawled over."

"No one dared look, while crossing, at those wild raging waters, leaping off that high cliff a few feet to the left."

Just how high is Bear Creek Falls? I do not know. Various pieces of promotional literature quote figures from 277 feet to 400 feet. Anyway it is high! Today with a wide cement structure spanning the top of the falls, most travelers have no idea of the depth below or of the vista that awaits if only they would stop to enjoy.

Many who do stop think that what they are observing is the wispy stream of water that falls hundreds of feet downward on the opposite side of the Uncompahgre Canyon. Many do not even see Bear Creek Falls itself, obscured by a twist in the highway and the depth protected by a stout wire fence.

But that wispy, lovely stream of water that forms the opposite falls has a strange story. Not even the name for that falls can be agreed upon. To some it is "Bridal Veil." To others it is "Horsetail or "Mares Tail." But there is a third name that goes back to a very old Indian legend. It is a story my father heard from the Utes who at one time traded with him in the Cascade Grocery on Main Street. Here is the story they told:

To the Utes, the bowl that is now Ouray was a sacred, medicinal retreat. Here they could bathe in the hot springs, take hot mud baths, and with the aid of their medicine man, find relief from many of their aches and pains. It was a site to be guarded and protected against intruders.

According to this tale, another Indian tribe found its way into the Ouray valley and there enjoyed the hot springs and the profusion of wild game. While they were enjoying themselves, the Utes, coming from down the valley, found them and it was war.

The larger body of Utes quickly drove the smaller hunting party of the other tribe back and upward along the deep canyon of the Uncompahgre. Finally in desperation the intruding tribe sent their women and children scrambling up the walls of the canyon while their braves made a last stand against the superior Utes. While their men fought to their death on the canyon floor, the women and children standing high above the canyon edge wept as they watched. Their tears formed that waterfall across the canyon from the lookout point of Bear Creek.

This is a story that I have never heard outside of our family which learned it from one of the elderly Utes who passed through Ouray seventy years ago. The Ute name for the falls was "Indian Tears."

The trachyte wall opposite Bear Creek Falls is seen by many summer visitors but many prefer the name the Utes gave it - Indian Tears.
— AUTHOR'S COLLECTION

CHAPTER 26

THE GOOD OLD DAYS?

Growing up seventy five years ago was a lot different than growing up today. We had virtually no organized activities for boys and girls or for youth in Ouray. Our parents couldn't place us in front of a television set to act as babysitter. We largely made our own amusements with the encouragement of parents.

Every evening our neighborhood was transformed into one large magnificent playground where we played games of "Red Light", "Kick the Can" and "Hide and Go Seek". The neighbors were generous with the use of their yards which became a part of our playing fields. In return we respected flower and garden beds.

Of course a good bit of our time was taken up carrying out "chores." Nearly every family in town kept a few chickens in a chicken yard back of the house. Many of us also had rabbit hutches. Chickens had to be fed, eggs brought to the house and feathers plucked after a hen was killed for Sunday dinner. Rabbits had to be fed, their hutches cleaned and fresh bedding spread. Of course young bunnies needed a bit of cuddling too. If there was a family horse or burro, that meant fetching it from the mountain side where it pastured overnight, currying and feeding it and in the evening turning it out again on the mountainside.

Carpets had to be beaten with the wire carpet beater — one family necessity we can be happy has long been forgotten. Girls had dusting to do, tables to be set, and beds to be made. When fruit became available, we all helped pick from the fruit trees in the yard. All fruit, whether from our own trees or bought from the farmers down valley who brought their produce to be hawked up and down the streets, had to be cleaned and processed. Cherries had to be pitted with a hair pin stuck into a cork and apples peeled, quartered and cored. Peeling peaches and removing the pits meant our arms were juice — covered up to (and sometimes above) our elbows. Gardens had to be weeded and tended. The produce from our own garden was an important part of our family meals and sustenance.

In those days the streets of Ouray were lined with trees. There were great tall trees, largely box elder, along Main Street, and today I would think my memory faulty if it wasn't for photographs that still exist of Main Street before the Colorado Highway Department attacked the trees with chain saws and the road with machinery to widen it. The result of their efforts is the plunging pavement on the west side of the street which still entraps unwary motorists attempting to park in the winter amid ice and snow.

In those far-away days, many of the streets were still lined with boardwalks, and boardwalks even existed along some portions of Main Street. For example a boardwalk was still present along the vacant lots between Sorenson's Feed Store (now the Cascade Deli) and the Cascade Grocery (now Pricco's Restaurant). I suppose it still existed as boardwalk at the time because of the dip at that point. It was expensive to fill it as was done later to create a base for a cement walk.

As a boardwalk in that particularly heavy traffic area, it offered an excellent opportunity for the town's boys, who were looking for the occasional coin that had fallen between the boards to the depression below. It was an opportunity that should be checked out whenever we went that way. And there was a vicarious thrill as we scrounged in the dirt looking for coins when a lady passed overhead, and we could gaze up in the hopes of seeing the forbidden. Unfortunately, the boards were so wide and the cracks so narrow all we had were imaginations to expand when telling our friends about our adventure.

The boardwalks in front of the Presbyterian Church were always a hoped for bonanza, because children did often drop a penny or a nickel when on their way to Sunday School. It was about an "even-steven" chance that the coin would bounce into one of the cracks. We didn't have the money for gum to put on the end of a stick to "fish" for the dropped coin. Instead we would chew a hunk of tar until it was soft enough to pick up the errant penny, work it on the end of a stick and go "fishing."

Another source of income was to collect the foil from wrappers which in that day and time kept products fresh. Tinfoil covered candy bars, the contents of cigar boxes, and many products that came from the grocery store. We scrounged for this foil in the "dumps" that were in various locations along the flumes that carried water from the two little streams that spouted down the mountainside to flow through town.

After collecting enough tinfoil to make a pressed ball at least as big as a softball, we would dig a depression in the ground big enough to surround the tinfoil ball. We would dig pitch from the pine trees and place it in the hole and then light the pitch. The more sophisticated efforts included digging a trench to a lower hole where the tinfoil would flow as it was melted. The product could then be carried to the man who operated the secondhand store on Main Street who would offer us a dime, if the resulting brick was of sufficient size. It took an awful lot of tinfoil to melt down to an acceptable brick. Some of the older boys got the idea of melting the tinfoil around the smallest of the iron balls used in the mills to crush ore. This did increase the weight of the brick, but the man who bought that ball never "bit" again, and he refused to buy another tin from them, leaving this market to the younger and more innocent.

Box Cañon (yes, always spelled without the "y") was a major tourist attraction, and it was touted in the booklets that the D& RG Railroad published to attract tourists. The City of Ouray had erected a huge sign, illuminated at night with many lightbulbs to draw the tourists to Box Cañon. The sign, although not lit, still exists on the far (west) side of the Cañon, high enough to be seen in most of the city. Money to erect and construct the sign was raised by the local merchants and was a considerable cost for that day. The week after the sign was built some citizens complained in the two local newspapers that "CAÑON" should be spelled with a "Y" (the traditional spelling, which was the way the sign was made, was just going out of use; Cañon City still uses the old form). Their complaints soon withered away when the merchants said they would be glad to make the change if those complaining would put up the money. The subject was dropped. Sixty years later new residents of Ouray complained that the sign was a blight on the beauty that surrounds Ouray, and the City Council, heeding their complaints, stopped its lighting. If lighted today it would be another charming reminder of the Victorian roots of the community.

But to return to my boyhood. The placing of the sign on top of the precipitous cliff offered a challenge a boy could not overlook. We had to climb that cliff to get to the sign, remove bulbs and throw them

Author Roger Henn's kindergarten class posed for this photograph in mid-winter about 1925. No one worried about coats on such a bright, sunny day.
— AUTHOR'S FAMILY COLLECTION

down the three hundred feet to the canyon floor. As I look at that cliff today, I cannot imagine how we scaled it without a rope and sophisticated climbing gear. But climb it we did—not often, but enough to raise the ire of the city fathers who had to replace the bulbs. I should note there was an easier route by taking the old road (now closely followed by the road to the head of the Oak Creek trail) which led to the Wood Ranch. It was called the Wood Ranch, for in earlier times wood for many of the town's wood-burning stoves came from there.

Hanging 260 feet high above the Box Cañon is the High Bridge. It is still a good climb for tourists who are determined to follow the rugged trail and many flights of stairs. The attraction to my gang was the railing on the bridge. Walking that railing from one end of the bridge to the other was an assignment that determined a good deal of the pecking order of our gang. Today, when I look down at that terrible drop I am amazed at how many of us managed to walk it and then laugh about it.

Bill Van Dome was in a group of boys several years older than my group, and he was a daredevil, accomplishing all sorts of risky things so that the rest of us stood in awe of him. One day he came upon the idea of walking the railing over the High Bridge, and he did it with grace and ease. Thus came the challenge that if any of us were to truly "belong," we also must walk the rail. I still remember the day that the gang decided it was my turn. As frightened as I was, I scrambled up to the rail and teetered back and forth with head and shoulders over the chasm. Three of us made it that day — Chuck Winnerah, Jimmy Gannon and myself. Jimmy's brother Tommy did try but jumped to the saftey of the bridge after a few steps - not quite as daring as his brother but a lot more brainy than the three of us who did make it.

The High Bridge had initially been built to carry a water pipe-line. Soon after its construction Ouray made it a wonderful summer Sunday afternoon walk by building access from the park over a long flight of stairs and a trail. The water pipeline was blasted through the wall of rock to create a tunnel for the line, and the popular trail hung on the hillside above the canyon and then moved inward to cross Oak Creek on a long swinging bridge. The trail then ended at what we called the "Old Reservoir," now referred to as the site of the West Reservoir. Now it is empty, but then it was filled with spar-kling water and a great rock which offered a diving site for the young people who foolishly dared to plummet into the cold, cold water. It wasn't for me; that water was just too cold.

I much preferred the water that came from the canyon floor and the old tunnel of the Trout and Fisherman. The hot water from that tunnel later heated the municipal swimming pool, but then it gurgled out from the tunnel, down over the rocks to join the waters of Can-yon Creek. Inside the tunnel an excavation some yards back from the entrance held a fairly good-sized pool of very hot water. It was so hot that one only plunged into it for a minute or so before climb-ing out as red as a beet. The joy of doing so was to do the forbidden.

After the long winter spring was most eagerly looked forward to. The hillside south of town where the ski tow and many houses now exist was then mostly barren of habitation, and the hillside bloomed with the color of the crocus, spring beauties and buttercups. Those flowers we picked to carry home and to school. On May Day we constructed baskets made from wallpaper books, filled them with flowers and early on May Day morning we carried them to hang on the doorknobs of neighbors and friends.

No, we never complained of having nothing to do — not with chores always awaiting and the hillsides to climb and fill the rest of our day.

CHAPTER 27

HOW TO FRIGHTEN A BEAR

When I was a young man way back in the 1930s, the surrounding hills still contained hundreds of great stumps left from the mining days of the 1880s. Logs were needed, not only for building cabins and mining buildings in the new mining camps, but also for timbering the new tunnels and shafts being dug. And the cutting of timber went on all year long, not only in the summer time. But when winter came the snow accumulated deeper and deeper in the high Rockies.

One "tenderfoot" who came to Red Mountain Town to live with her husband, a mining engineer, arrived in the summer and was amazed at the high stumps of eight or so feet that surrounded the new camp. When she asked why the stumps were so high, she was told because the trees had been cut in the winter and the men were working in snow six to eight feet deep, so the trees were cut accordingly. She was certain that as a tenderfoot they were "pulling her leg," but she found out differently when winter came.

This phenomenon occurred not only in Red Mountain but throughout the early mining camps of the San Juans. And so it was at Animas Forks, where the mountainside above the town was sprinkled with great stumps. All have since rotted away, and the tourist of today has no inkling that 120 years ago, this was a mountainside of virgin forest.

It was on this mountainside that I was hiking one day in 1936. Because of the heavy fallen timber, I was having difficulty in seeing my way when I came upon a particularly great stump. It was fully eight feet tall and perhaps four feet in diameter; indeed it had been a most noble tree. What a good place to climb and overlook the valley, I thought, and so I set out to climb that old scarred and beaten stump.

Up I climbed, clinging to the old knotted places where limbs had been broken off some fifty years before when the tree had been cut. Finally on top, it proved to be hollow, all rotted out inside, and I straddled the rotted center, one foot either side of the hole. Somehow I slipped — perhaps the rotten spot was a bit wider than I thought, and my left foot slipped down into that hole. Of course I threw my weight onto my right foot, but that proved to be too rotted also, and down I went into the cavity of that tree.

As I went down my hands and arms were forced into the air and down, down I went to such a depth my hands did not quite reach the top of the stump, and because of various knobs that stuck out inside the cavity, I did not sink deep enough so my feet could touch bottom.

Of course as I hung there I shouted a few times in a panic and then reason began to return. Who was nearer than a mile or so to hear my cries? How were my companions to guess where I had rambled on that afternoon? What to do? Well I did what I do best, I dozed off.

I was awakened by the sound of something rubbing in the brush outside. My first reaction was to holler for help, but then I realized it sounded more like an animal than a human and perhaps yelling wasn't the thing to do. Then came a scratching and clawing on the outside of the stump, and the hole over my head was blocked from the light. From the smell, I knew the newcomer must be a bear. He must have been using the stump as a den to hibernate in and was coming back to rest after a successful day of hunting for grubs and berries.

I didn't have to do any thinking; that bear was settling and beginning to back down in the hole. I pulled my arms back down the little I could, and when he reached my hands I grabbed the hair on his rump and yelled as loud as I could. Well old bruin jumped high in the air, and I hung on for dear life. He jerked me high enough so I could get my elbows over the rim of the hole as he jumped down off the stump and ran off through the fallen woods and bushes at full speed.

Well that is one way to frighten a bear.

Encounters with bears could happen at any time. This prospector has met his match on a narrow mountain trail.
— COURTESY OF P. DAVID SMITH
— FRANK LESLIE'S ILLUSTRATED NEWSPAPER, FEBRUARY 13, 1886

CHAPTER 28

HOW NOT TO HIKE HORSE THIEF TRAIL

Half encircling the beautiful bowl that is the setting for Ouray, winds the Horse Thief Trail. It is truly a trail of history, possibly the oldest in Colorado and one of the oldest in the United States. It antedates the arrival of American gold hunters, mountain men and the Spanish. How old it is, we can only guess.

The trail abruptly climbs from near the swimming pool up into the eastern cliffs. In a short mile (as the trail is measured) it gains a half mile in altitude — and that mile traversed is the longest mile you will ever hike. The trail switches back and forth through the Blowout, which is half of the crater of an extinct volcano, the other half having been blown out into the valley of the Uncompahgre. From the distance it is beautiful in its shades of colors ranging from whites and grays to yellows and reds. But traveling through that absolutely barren half bowl when the sun is shining is a reasonable resemblance to a trip through Dante's Inferno.

When I was a boy this trail was called the Gold Hill Trail, for it led to the fabulously rich mines on Gold Hill - the American Nettie, the Wankah and others. The only access to these mines was via the Gold Hill Trail, a part of the Horse Thief Trail. It was always a trail and never transformed into a road. In the morning the long strings of mules and burros would almost fill the street in front of the old Cascade Grocery (now Pricco's Restaurant) as the animals were packed with food for the boarding houses, powder and other supplies for the mines. On hot summer days the pack trains were clouded with dust; on rainy days the mud stuck to the hooves of the animals who would grow impatient and kick or bite an unwary packer. Finally with burdens properly disbursed, the animals would be strung out to begin the hard climb up the Gold Hill Trail. The mules were in strings of fifteen or twenty and tied head to tail and led by a mule skinner. The burros were driven in herds by the burro punchers, so named for the sticks they carried and used like a spear on lagging animals.

Somewhere, up in the distances of the blowout, the Gold Hill Trail branches off, and the Horse Thief continues onward to the crest of what the locals call "The Overlook." Then it continues going eastward along the crest of the mountains.

An old Indian once told me the usual beginning of Horse Thief for the Utes was at Buckhorn Lake. He also told of a gold cache the Ute Indians made near where the trail begins at Buckhorn. He said the gold came from a mine the Spanish were working centuries ago. When Indians found them, they drove them from the country, killing some of the miners, taking their gold, carrying it along the Horse Thief Trail and burying it near Buckhorn Lake. It's a good story and very plausible, but without more specifics the area is just too large to be searched successfully. How the beginning of the trail changed from Buckhorn to the part of the Horse Thief that we know today, I haven't the faintest idea; I've never tried to locate it.

Today the commonly used path to the Horse Thief goes opposite Old Bachelor Switch (now called Whispering Pines). Before the abandonment of the old narrow gauge railroad, a spur ran off from the mainline, and freight cars could be left there to load the ore from Bachelor Mine. A county road now runs steeply up the opposite side of Highway 550 past the lovely Lake Lenore, then along Red Rock Creek (as it was called in the early years until changed to Dexter Creek) to the site of the Old Bachelor Mine. At one time this was a fabulous silver producer and the townsite of Ash, whose name came from the first letters of the last names of the three bachelors who discovered the mine. At one time Ash had its own school house, post office, livery stable, saloon and store as well as a large mill. A flood rushing down Dexter Creek washed away most of the buildings. The digging of the Syracuse Tunnel at a lower elevation resulted in tearing down of what remained of old Ash. If you range up and down amid the forest you will come across ruins of the miners' houses and an occasional larger ruin that must have been a boarding house or restaurant. For years we have taken table linens, crystal and china and have enjoyed an evening eating out in a cabin on the hillside overlooking Ash that we think must have housed a restaurant.

From Ash onward the road becomes one for jeeps. It switches back through the spruce forest until it ends at the Wedge Mine. From

These riders are silhouetted on the part of the Horse Thief Trail that is called the "Bridge of Heaven." There is no doubt that heaven is where you will be if your horse makes a wrong step. — Courtesy of P. David Smith

there it becomes a trail that is marked by a Forest Service sign, "2 miles to Horse Thief Trail."

This trail is well marked and leads through a hillside of gigantic aspen. After climbing at least two miles and most of an hour, the hiker comes upon a second sign which says exactly the same thing, "Horse Thief Trail — 2 miles." Soon however, the trail from the Wedge joins the trail from the swimming pool at a point very near the overlook which can be gained by only a short hike.

From this point the trail winds up and down until the "Bridge of Heaven" is reached. This is a narrow knife-edged ridge with paralyzing drop-offs on either side and just about the grandest view of all the Rockies. Here a word of warning — more than one unwary traveler has been killed by lightning on the "Bridge of Heaven." As a boy I can well remember seeing canvas-wrapped bodies being carried by horses from the Bridge of Heaven to Ouray's Main Street.

The trail then climbs up and down and through meadows along the eastern edge of the Amphitheater until it reaches the treeless American Flats — not really flat at all, but compared to the 13,000 to 14,000 peaks ranging around it, the undulating tundra surface is flat. Here the trail becomes entwined with trails made by the great sheep herds that graze the area, and with a lack of trail signs the novice can easily become lost.

Many years ago I set out with my family and seventy-year-old Tom Gallagher for a pleasant day hike to complete a hiking merit badge for our son. We intended to follow Horse Thief Trail from the Wedge up and over the Bridge of Heaven and across American Flats to the Engineer road where a jeep was to meet us. As it was a pleasant summer day, we were dressed lightly, some in shorts, and we carried only light day packs. All went marvelously well, and we made good time crossing the Bridge of Heaven and rounding the trail over the headwaters of Cascade Creek. But when we reached the American Flats, it began to rain, clouds descended around us, and we could no longer see the landmarks of the peaks which we had expected to guide us. The many trails made by the sheep herds confused us, and we lost the Horse Thief Trail. We finally climbed a peak to see if we could locate where we were. Old Tom saw an old road far below and plunged downward to reach it. Our shouts to dissuade him went unanswered, and we were forced to follow, for we couldn't let the old gentleman go off by himself. Down we plunged on the grassy mountainside until we caught up with Tom and found ourselves at the headwaters of Bear Creek. The downpour made the creek such a torrent it was impossible to cross and follow that trail down to safety.

For a little while we took refuge from the rain in an old cabin which still remained at the Yellow Jacket Mine ruins. An outhouse was still standing, and we all took turns using it. The last person to use the falling down facility was my sister. She disappeared inside and was gone for a very long time. We became concerned, and my wife went to see what was detaining her. What had happened was that she had pulled her very wet jeans down to use the facilities, and then because they had shrunk could not pull them back up again. The two women struggled and struggled and finally succeeded in pulling them on, but fastening them was out of the question. She was forced to complete the adventure with her jeans unzipped.

Unable to go further down Bear Creek Trail, the only alternative was to climb back up to American Flats. As it was getting very late in the afternoon there was a question as to whether or not we could get to Engineer Pass in time to meet the jeep. But we set out, leaving the only protection from the weather that was available for miles.

The couple of miles that we spent climbing out of the awful "hole" were a horror. We literally pulled the seventy-year-old man who was with us up that distance. When we started out we would count 500 steps and then stop to rest. Then it was 400, then 300 and finally twenty-five. By the time we reached American Flats, daylight was fast disappearing. We struggled along with cloud cover limiting our vision and going toward what we hoped was the right place. After dark hit we crept — and I do mean crept — onward very carefully so as to be sure we didn't tumble off the edge of what seemed to be the ancient road we were following.

It simply was too dangerous. We had nothing to eat, and our efforts to build a fire on the treeless and woodless American Flats were unsuccessful. Finally we spread one of the two ponchos we had on the ground, lay down upon it in very close communion and tried to cover ourselves with the other. With six in the party, the two on the outside ended up with very little cover.

It was a most miserable night as we lay shivering and shaking in our soaked clothing. Sometimes the stars would come out and then disappear, as a new shower resoaked us. As soon as daylight began we were up and moving in an attempt to get warm. The low clouds had gone, and we could see a great distance over the flats. The disintegrating road we had been following was on the side of the mountain that would forty years later be named Darley Mountain.

A considerable distance away we could see a herd of sheep in a bowl on the side of Engineer Mountain. Obviously, we were in a bad way. Two of the party were hypothermic. We left them with the remaining two who were still in fair condition, and my son Alan and I started a long distant run to seek help from the sheepherders. Then we saw one of the herders on horseback heading across the flats, and we ran to intercept him and finally did. He turned out not to speak English, and the only Spanish that I could remember from my high school days was "Habla usted español?" He replied volubly, and we couldn't understand a word. He couldn't understand us either. Finally when I asked if he could tell us where the jeep road was, a smile crossed his face and he enthusiastically pointed saying, "Jeep, Jeep." So we had learned where the jeep road was that came off of Engineer Pass.

We continued on our way, running to reach the sheepherder camp, but much to our shock, the crew was breaking camp, packing their horses and urging the sheep up over Engineer Mountain via what we later learned was the old pass used before the days of jeeps. They were gone before we could catch up with them. It turned out the sheep were being grazed in an area where they were not supposed to be, and when they saw us running toward them, the herders panicked thinking we might be rangers.

Without that help we returned to the rest of the party for consultation. It was agreed that we must seek help, and Alan and I started out again alternating between a trot and a run to reach the road leading up Engineer Pass. We were fearful of how far we would have to run before finding help which we needed badly.

To our joy we eventually saw a jeep coming down from the pass. Two old friends who were very concerned at our failure to show the night before had come to the rescue. The two of us climbed aboard and rode down off the pass to where the rest of the party was slowly approaching. The best news was that our rescuers had a gallon of hot soup.

We were indeed most fortunate, because this occurred many years before the organization of mountain rescue units. This experience leads me to urge and warn all who take this trail to go well prepared and not be as foolish as we were.

CHAPTER 29 🔥

JUSTIFIABLE HOMICIDE

The life of a prospector was a lonely one. Any time spent in town was lost time in his search for a hoped-for bonanza. His search was a solitary one and, jealously, he did not welcome others while he was prospecting. Many of the old-time prospectors abandoned their search for wealth when the snows of winter began to fall and sought the warmth and fellowship of the towns of the San Juans. However if his summer's work had resulted in finding a promising outcrop of vein, the prospector most probably would build a rude shelter and spend the winter developing his prospect. Such was the case of "Old Clint" (for some reason all prospectors were referred to as "young" or "old" but never "middle-aged"; actually Clint was in his forties, but that was considered old in the times of the early San Juans).

Clint had found what appeared to be a promising outcropping in Silver Basin, high above Porters which was to later become the community of Sneffels. Stone was aplenty in that high basin, so the shack he constructed was largely built of stone with logs for the roof beams and rough sawn boards for the roof. It was a crude shelter furnished only with a rough bunk against the far wall, a stove for heat and cooking and a small plank table with a powder keg for a chair. There Clint was to spend the winter; his nearest neighbor perhaps two miles away and separated by high mountain ridges and a twenty foot depth of snow. While the snow increased his isolation, as it piled around his rock shelter it provided needed insulation from frigid winds that swept over and around his barren dwelling. The shack was so constructed that it covered the mouth of the prospect hole he was digging, so he had no need to go outside and into the frozen world in order to continue his exploration.

Snow comes early to the high San Juans, and by mid-October Clint was isolated from civilization — such as it was — at Porter's store. It would be many a month before he could again talk with another human being. Many such isolated men confined to a small space developed "cabin fever" — hallucinations, among other things.

Sidney Basin in the summer is a beautiful spot but the old miner's cabin in this story probably looked something like this in the winter. There was snow, snow and more snow.
— AUTHOR'S FAMILY COLLECTION

Clint had been confined in his icy cage for some weeks, when one day he heard and saw a buzzing fly. Now to many of us the first response would be to swat the creature. But to Clint this fly was the only live creature he would see for months, and he welcomed its company. He would place a sugar cube on his table not far from his plate, since in reality, he usually ate from his frying pan. The fly would settle on the sugar cube, and Clint would hold a conversation with his cabin mate. Thus the long winter weeks and months passed by. When Clint sat to eat at his crude table the fly would join him on the sugar cube and Clint enjoyed many one-sided conversations with his pal.

At last an early spring thaw began, and one afternoon a prospector from over the ridge came by on his way down to Porter's. He was on his long Norwegian snowshoes . . . twelve or fifteen feet in length, the predecessor to our modern skis and the mode of transportation of those unfortunate to have to travel in the high San Juans during the winter. Clint welcomed him and invited him to spend the night. Soon the two were engaged in a lively conversation which carried on as they prepared their evening meal.

They sat down for supper, and as it had been trained to do, the fly flew to join them and settled on its cube of sugar. Clint's guest promptly swatted and killed the fly. Clint, enraged over the death of his pet, reached behind him, grabbed the gun that stood in the corner and shot and killed the visitor.

The next morning Clint took the skis that once had belonged to his visitor and skied the long slopes downward to Porter's Store. A party from the settlement set out and retrieved the body, carrying it down to Ouray, where it rests in an unmarked grave in Cedar Hill Cemetery.

A coroner's jury was convened at Porter's. Clint told his story, and the six men who composed the jury considered the evidence. They were men who understood the loneliness of the remote mines and prospects. Unlike you and me, they could understand the close relationship that had developed between Clint and his pet fly. The jury found "justifiable homicide," and Clint trudged back to his lonesome shack to spend the remainder of the winter. The findings of the coroner's jury can be found in the old records in the basement of the Ouray County Courthouse.

CHAPTER 30 🌿

ROMANCE & ADVENTURE IN THE EARLY SAN JUANS

The romance began while traveling on a wagon train. It was a wagon train that crossed the Great Plains populated by Indians and buffalo, and it was headed for Pike's Peak during the gold rush of 1859. On the road to Pike's Peak that toiling wagon train was not alone in crossing the vast plains, for as many as 150,000 gold seekers made that 1859 trek to answer to the call of "Gold!"

Mary Melissa Nye was a young mother, who with her two small children, accompanied her husband Nathan Nye. Mary Melissa had been married at an early age to a man much older. In fact at age thirteen her twenty-six-year old husband was twice her age. The Nyes came from New York State.

Married at such an early age, Mary Melissa had never had the opportunity to enjoy the romance of courting, so perhaps it was only to be expected that her eye soon caught the handsome young Charles L. Hall. Hall had been destined by his family to become a Presbyterian minister. But instead of enrolling in a Presbyterian seminary, young Hall bought a flour mill in Maquoketa, Iowa. The mill burned and Hall, seeking to replenish his purse, joined the wagon train that included Mary Melissa Nye.

But Nathan Nye kept a close eye on his impressionable young wife and made sure there was no opportunity for romance. So at the time the wagon train arrived in Aurora, nothing untoward had happened, although we may be sure that Charles Hall and Mary Melissa Nye were very much aware of each other.

After a long, hard winter in Denver-Aurora, the spring of 1860 finally came, and many of the wagon train heard the call of new discoveries in the heart of the Rocky Mountains. So a sizable party went on from Cherry Creek to cross South Park, climb over hazardous Mosquito Pass and go on to new discoveries at Buckskin Joe in California Gulch near present-day Leadville. Nathan Nye, his wife and two children, were in this party as well as his brother F. A. Nye and his family. This group also included some of the most influential people from the

This early day drawing of Baker's Park makes the mountains only slightly steeper than they really are. It was wild and rugged country in 1875, and it still is! — COURTESY OF P. DAVID SMITH — FRANK LESLIE'S ILLUSTRATED NEWSPAPER. MAY 8, 1875

Cherry Creek camp — D. H. and Bell Haywood, Stephen B. Kellogg and F. R. Rice, to name a few. The party arrived in Buckskin Joe (where H. A. W. Tabor carried the official title of postmaster while Augusta carried out the actual duties and also ran their small store while Tabor prospected for gold). Shortly after arriving in the camp, Mary Melissa became seriously ill. According to an account written in later years by her daughter from her second marriage, Mary Melissa was abandoned by her husband Nate who took their two children. Possibly he assumed that the ill Mary Melissa was dying and would not recover; nevertheless he abandoned her and thus became thoroughly despicable. He later wrote to her that the two children he had taken with him had died shortly after he left her.

In the summer of 1860 Charles Baker arrived in Buckskin Joe to seek a "stake" and to lead an expedition into the San Juan Mountains to look for silver and gold. With backing from Stephen B. Kellogg and F. R. Rice, Baker soon began his first venture into the San Juans leading a party of six. Baker was not by any means the first prospector in the San Juans, but it was his written reports and newspaper accounts that excited the "rush to the San Juans". That fall Baker returned again with an expedition that this time totaled about 150.

Numerous other stories of the San Juans appeared, most of them negative as to their appraisal of instant wealth. Nevertheless, new expeditions began enthusiastically, including that of Doc Arnold which left Denver in the early fall of 1860. Later, 200 men, women, and children headed for the San Juans from Denver in December

1860. This party was headed by Kellogg and his family, and is often mistakenly referred to as the "Baker Expedition," although Baker was not a member, and his only remote relationship to the party was the financial aid he had received months earlier from Kellogg and F. R. Rice, also a member of the December expedition. D. H. Haywood (who was the most prominent member of the wagon train coming to Denver in 1859) and his family were members of the party, and his presence may have attracted the family of F. A. Nye and his sister-in-law Mary Melissa Nye. She may have traveled with F. A. Nye or with the Haywoods, as Belle Haywood was her close friend. And surprise, also in the party was Charles L. Hall.

Leaving in the winter, the trip to the San Juans must have been most difficult. In all probability the Kellogg wagon party joined up with one led by Thomas Pollock who had eleven army wagons, each pulled by six or eight yoke of oxen. He carried a stock of basic groceries and tools and drove 200 head of cattle. The large party slugged south along the Front Range, but when they began crossing the Sangre De Christo Mountains it took eleven days to go from LaVeta (on the east end of the pass) to the area where Fort Garland was situated.... a distance of fifteen miles. Finally they arrived at Animas City in the southern San Juans in the middle of March.

Animas City had been founded the previous year at the head of the lovely Animas Valley, at a point now called Pinkerton Springs. From there some of the men wintering at Animas City together with men from the new arrivals would climb over the mountains to Baker's Park. There is no evidence that any woman or child entered the park that was to eventually become Silverton. The route to Baker's Park did not follow today's highway over Molas Divide but went up Cascade Creek and down Bear Creek (past today's Bear Mountain) where Mineral Creek led into Baker's Park. The search for gold was centered at the upper end of the park at the site that would eventually become Eureka. The trail was most hazardous. Those who traveled early enough in the late winter had been able to move across on the top of the hard snow, but those in the spring faced greater difficulties as the deep snow softened.

Somewhere around fifty to seventy-five men started out with intention of shoveling out the trail to make it easier for stock to travel. But overnight the shoveled trail was filled with new snow. The next night the same thing happened. Snowshoes became the means of travel.

Charlie Hall was among the first of the snowshoe travelers and later told of taking horses over the trail, although he found it necessary to shovel his way through snow drifts and to pack snow in ravines to provide a trail for the animals. Despite these efforts, eight of the animals fell from the trail and were killed.

Those going into the San Juans were equipped only to search for gold in the way gold had been found at Cherry Creek and earlier in California — that was, by panning or using sluice boxes. They knew little of hard rock mining and had no equipment to undertake such a task. Their search consisted of looking for gold at their feet, and they failed to look up and around them at the silver veins that were discernable in the high mountains – minerals which would have made them wealthy had they but looked and had the tools to develop the veins. They tried to get to the gold in the gravel, but melting snow and runoff promptly filled their diggings. One group worked a week and reported only $1.25 in gold. With such little success, the men began going further and higher into the mountains looking for the elusive gold as the snow melted.

And so it was that Charlie Hall with two companions, Dick Harris and Miles O'Neal, set out to look in the Uncompahgre watershed. Others had gone into the gulches at the headwaters looking for placer gold and overlooking the lode deposits of quartz outcroppings, but only one party had gone down the Uncompahgre itself. A party that included Nate Hurd had descended as far as Ouray's Bear Creek Canyon where steep cliffs had foiled their efforts to cross. Probably both the Hall and Hurd parties had learned of the Uncompahgre Valley from others now at either Animas City or the diggings at Eureka. These would have included George Howard and members of the Doc Arnold Party, all of whom had come through that area in 1860.

Hall and his two companions from Eureka, climbed up Eureka Gulch and crossed over to the Uncompahgre Canyon; the cliffs were so steep and jagged that the party found the going easier by wading down the ragging torrent rather than attempting to follow the canyon from the rim above. When they reached the waterfall where the Uncompahgre plunges down to join Red Mountain Creek, (the point that old-timers call State Bridge and where today's four wheelers take off from the Million Dollar Highway at Engineer Pass) the party turned north and followed the cliff edge until they reached the abandoned camp established by Nate Hurd a few days earlier. This was at Bear Creek Canyon where the Hurd Party had turned back unable to find a way of crossing.

Where Hurd and his associates failed, Hall and his party succeeded. At this time the lanky Hall was called by the nickname "Squirrel," and the appropriateness of the name now became apparent. One man stood on another's shoulders while Hall climbed this living pole and was able to seize a branch that hung over the chasm and swing himself so he could drop on the opposite cliff's edge. There he was able to cut a tree so that it fell across the torrent so that his companions could cross.

The party climbed down into the present site of Ouray, and panning as they went, followed the Uncompahgre River downstream. As was true throughout the San Juans, panning resulted in little "color," and they had been unable to bring much in the way of supplies over the rough terrain they had come through. By the time they reached Cow Creek their food supplies were very low, so they realized they must return to Baker's Park to replenish their provisions. Going back the way they had come was sure to be most difficult, so they decided to strike east and locate the Los Pinos River by which trails would lead them to large encampments. As modern day climbers and hikers can testify, following Cow Creek is most difficult and virtually impossible to cross for a poorly equipped party. Lost, and their food gone, the three determined that the best bet was to return to the Uncompahgre and locate the abandoned Doc Arnold camp where they knew hides had been left. They hoped the hides would provide enough nourishment to give them strength to attempt to reach the camp at Eureka.

Thoroughly lost, they could not find Arnold's camp. They boiled flour sacks and drank the resulting broth. They ate their boot tops, buckskin breeches and a buffalo robe they carried for warmth at night. They abandoned almost all their equipment except a pistol used to start fires. Ants in a dead log proved a delicacy as they wandered lost, confused and in paranoia.

Each became concerned that the other two planned to kill and eat him. In fear of his life, O'Neal took off on his own and somehow did reach Baker's Park, and immediately left the area. The other two struggled on, weaker and weaker. To arise they had to lie on their faces and work to a standing posture using their elbows. Towards the last it was a matter of crawling on their hands and knees. A day of great effort often resulted in a distance so slight they could still see where they started.

Their memory of the final day is confused. Certainly they expected to die where they collapsed. For some reason Hall, who was carrying the pistol, fired — perhaps to start a fire. A group of four men from the Baker's Park group were crossing Engineer Mountain while returning from a prospecting trip to the Lake Fork area. They heard the shot, investigated, and found Hall unconscious and Harris delirious and snow-blind. Hall's legs were so frozen a pin could be stuck in them without the slightest reaction, recalled Ben Eaton, one of the rescuing party of four.

Hall's legs were packed in snow, and fortunately a grouse was killed and a broth prepared which was fed him spoonful by spoonful. The two were carried out by the rescue party, down the long trail (through the future communities of Mineral Point and Animas Fork) to where the Baker's Park camp was located (probably at either the later site of Eureka or Howardsville). Hall was weighed, and found that together with overcoat and clothes he totaled only forty eight pounds! There he was cared for until he could be carried on horseback to Camp Pleasant. Crops which were planted in plots near Animas City were fed to Hall and aided in his recovery. Mary Melissa took charge of his recovery which was amazingly swift. Undoubtedly his improvement was helped by the swelling of a love that had been forbidden during the crossing of the prairie in the wagon train two years before. To the delight of those in the encampment they were now witness to a marvelous love story unfolding. And who could have wished anything but the best to the brave young woman who had suffered abandonment by her husband and the death of her two children and to the remarkable young man who had survived hardships few could have lived through.

The end of the Baker venture into the San Juans was nearing a close. Everyone was the poorer in wealth from the undertaking. Untold numbers had been lost in the wilderness attempting to reach or leave Baker's Park and were never accounted for. The exodus began; Camp Pleasant ceased to exist, and the collection of log houses that formed Animas City was abandoned, to be again discovered nearly ten years later.

It seems Charlie Hall and his newly won love must have left with the remnants of the Kellogg-Pollack party which arrived at Fort Garland on July 4, 1861. And that brings our attention to another story of the Baker Days. News of the developing struggle between the North and the South reached the remote San Juans, and soon the families and would-be-miners were divided into disagreeing groups. Mary Melissa and her friend Belle Haywood and the wife of Orange Phelps made an American Flag. They used a red flannel dress, blue bonnets and some white yard goods originally intended to make a shroud. Exactly where it was flown is unknown, but by all accounts it was taken down by Confederate sympathizers. Mary Melissa later was to tell that it was returned to her by Kit Carson, but no amplification was given.

Mary Melissa and Charlie were married in 1862. Charlie served as lieutenant in the Second Colorado Volunteers. He later developed the South Park Salt Works. He was elected twice to the Colorado Territorial Legislature from Park County and once to the Colorado State Legislature. In addition to the Salt Works he became a partner of H.A.W. Tabor in Denver's Windsor Hotel, moved to Leadville where he was manager and president of that city's gas company and continued his interest in San Juan mining, although this activity did not prove lucrative. He did make a major discovery which became the Mammoth Mine in Arizona. He died in Denver in 1907.

That strong willed Mary Melissa, after marrying Charlie, had three children, one of whom wrote a romantic version of her mother's life. Mary Melissa eventually went blind and was severely lame by the time she reached forty. She became a founder of the Colorado Christian Science denomination and obtained almost complete relief from her rheumatism. She died in 1899. Charlie's only granddaughter became an actress over his objections, and he disinherited her. The granddaughter, Antoinette Perry, married F. W. Freauff and inherited his millions upon his death. She had become a well-known Broadway actress and the "Tony" Awards were named for her.

Interestingly Charlie's key rescuer from the tour into the Uncompahgre was Benjamin Harrison Eaton who became Colorado's fourth governor. Indeed an amazing number of those identified as a part of the "Baker" adventure were to return to the San Juans in later years.

Wouldn't this story make a wonderful movie?

CHAPTER 31 🌾

SILVERTON'S FIRST CAT

Cats were difficult to acclimatize in the Colorado Rockies, and this was particularly true of the San Juan towns which existed at high altitudes as compared to lower altitude communities where cats were not only healthy, but often overflowed those frontier towns. But the high San Juan communities wanted cats, not only for pets but to control the rodents which found easy living among the ramshackle dwellings.

So it was in Silverton. The early settlers had great difficulty in keeping the cats alive that were brought to that high altitude. According to historian Duane Smith, many of the stray cats that inhabited Durango's alleys and back yards were rounded up and brought to Silverton in an attempt to use them to reduce the population of pack rats and rock squirrels that were making free use of the oats and grain in the stables and then at night prowling the houses of the townspeople. Unfortunately the cats could not withstand the jump in altitude between Durango and Silverton.

But Smith failed to record the story of the old Tom that was the first to successfully acclimate to the altitude. He was a black and white (well, that white was usually very gray from the dirt beneath the packing box he called home) old Tom who had been the victor in many an alley brawl or singing contest held on backyard fences. He had lost one front leg in some alley brawl, and one of the hands at the stable, where he begged for food, had whittled out a wooden leg and successfully found a means of harnessing it to the Tom. After awhile he got used to the appendage and got along quite well as long as he kept off fence tops.

Having proven his ability to adjust to unusual and difficult conditions, old Tom was brought to Silverton, to be released to see if he could survive. Acclimate he did, and he became a real force for rats and squirrels to reckon with. He would lie in wait as motionless as he could behind a fence post or behind a door. When an unsuspecting rodent would run by, Old Tom would raise his peg leg and whack the unsuspecting creature in the head.

Indeed that old Tom was the joy of Silverton! His professional pursuit of the pack rats and rock squirrels put him in much demand. Old miners vied with one another to use his activities at their more-or-less junkie abodes. They attempted to bribe him with bits of bacon and sausage, "Oh, he began to live the "Life of Riley." In fact, the attempts to seduce him for his services led to old Tom no longer needing to catch rodents.

Then the unspeakable happened. Tom had been lured to the boarding house operated by the Byron Tafts. There in the pursuit of a warm place to sleep, he wandered into the bedroom where Baby Anna was sleeping. It was a fortunate happenstance, for a large rat had just climbed onto the bed and had begun to nip at little Anna's fingers. The parents, busy with feeding their boarders, paid no attention to her cries. But Tom did. He pounced on the nibbling rat and with his peg leg clubbed him to death.

Tom, already full from the treats earlier supplied by Mrs. Sarah Taft, did not need a further repast—what he needed was a warm place to sleep. So he cuddled under Anna's chin, his fur tickling the child to sleep again. When mother Taft came in to check on her baby there the two laid snuggled together (although Tom's peg leg was a little bloody), and further down on the bed was the battered rat. Tom was a hero!

While Tom kept the mice and rats away from the Taft boarding house, he never again had to scrounge around the rest of Silverton, for now he was a house cat, petted and loved by the town's first child, Anna Silverton Taft. When the Tafts later left Silverton to go to establish a boarding house at the lower altitude of the town of Dallas down along the Uncompahgre River, Old Tom went with Anna Silverton Taft, to live out the remainder of his life as a pampered lap cat.

This photograph shows the author's mother with his father's favorite cat, "Tommy." He was a large, "rough and tumble" cat who could well take care of himself.
— AUTHOR'S FAMILY COLLECTION

CHAPTER 32

HOW TO FIND A MINE — BY FISHING

Gus Begole and Jack Echoles are credited with finding and establishing modern day Ouray, first coming into the little valley in July 1875. After returning to Eureka, they came back to Ouray, and while out on the trail on August 11 met another party who were hunting and fishing who they told of their discovery. Begole and Echoles had found promising "float," and based on this had staked two claims, the Cedar and the Clipper. But they had not found the source of the "float."

The party that Begole and Echoles had met proceeded on to the site, and being short of supplies, Whitlock and Staley decided to go fishing, so as to add fresh fish to their depleted larder. Leaving companions Judge R. F. Long and Captain M. W. Cline behind to make camp in the wooded area that was to become Ohlwiler's Park, the two set off for the Uncompahgre River.

The Uncompahgre River carries a considerable flow of water from the drainage on the three Red Mountains. The pollution was great even in 1776 when the Fathers Escalante and Dominques came upon it, probably near present day Colona. When the Fathers asked their Ute guide the name of the river; he replied in grunts which the Fathers wrote down as Ancapagri; the Fathers called it the Rio de San Francisco. Their Ute guide explained the name Ancapagri was red water, "hot and bad tasting."

In the 1980s the EPA and the Colorado Health Department decided the Uncompahgre was too dirty. They placed the blame on mining , requiring the Idarado Mining Company to clean up the river that has, probably from the beginning of time and certainly at least as far back as 1776, been polluted by the natural flow of water from the heavily mineralized Red Mountains. No matter how extensive an effort is made, the Uncompahgre River will still be "red, hot and bad tasting."

It is not surprising that when the two fishermen reached the bank of the river and observed the reddish, nasty looking water that they turned and went up river to where the Uncompahgre was joined by the clear water of what we now call Canyon Creek. There they could see fish, and there they began their casting.

As they were fishing and scrambling alongside the racing water and pools of Canyon Creek, one of them observed shiny copper stains on the walls of the canyon opposite from where they were fishing. The two crossed over, sampled the wall and promptly abandoned fishing and began staking claims. Appropriately, they called the two claims they staked that day the Trout and the Fisherman.

The four "hunters and fishermen" left to return to Mineral Point the next day, carrying samples which Professor D. W. Brunton's assay found to be worth $30,000 a ton if all the ore was as rich as the selected samples. Encouraged, Whitlock and Staley roughed out a crude trail from Mineral Point (then called Mineral City by the hopeful boomers) back down to Ouray. They returned with sufficient burros to pack enough ore back up the rough trail to Mineral Point and sell it for $800.

With money in hand the two bought mining equipment and supplies at Del Norte. These they carried up the Rio Grande, over Stony Pass to Howardsville, up the Animas River to Mineral Point and then down their rough trail to the future site of Ouray and the location of the Trout and Fisherman claims.

Getting ready to work all winter on their claims, the two constructed one of the first of three cabins to be built in Ouray. Evidently their work was successful, for in December Abram Cutler and Long, who had brought wagons to Ouray, set out for Pueblo with a load of ore — the first major shipment to be made from Ouray.

By 1883 the claims had been sold to a group of investors headed by E.W. McIntyre, the first man elected to the Colorado legislature from the San Juans. The 1883 mining Directory of Colorado reported that the claims had been patented in 1881, with five shafts of from ten to fifty feet in depth, fifty feet of open cuts and thirty square feet of stoping with a probable output of $15,000.

As a youth, some years before Ouray's hot water swimming pool was constructed, we used to hike into the canyon to the old Trout tunnel which contained a large pool of hot water. We would shed our clothes and pretend we were going swimming (the water was too shallow for that, but it was very, very hot). When the municipal pool

The Trout and Fisherman mining claim was located just outside of Boy Canyon in Ouray, which would be in the right foreground of this early-day postcard
— COURTESY OF P. DAVID SMITH

was completed, this tunnel became the source of hot water for the pool.

An 1860 expedition, on its way to join the Baker parties along the Animas River, in what was to become Silverton, was caught by the snows of winter and the men wintered in the middle of the Uncompahgre Valley at the foot of Coal Creek on land that is now the San Juan Guest Ranch. They reported doing extensive prospecting in the nearby mountains and finding good mineral prospects at the head of the Uncompahgre, but the water was so hot they were forced to abandon their mining efforts. Quite possibly the "discovery" of the Trout and Fisherman" was a "rediscovery" of the workings of that 1860 expedition, and perhaps the two fisherman were attracted to the site by the old workings of fifteen years earlier.

One way to find a mine is to go fishing!

CHAPTER 33 🔥

COAL IS BETTER THAN GOLD?

John Porter had a coal field. In the year 1876 the question was how
to find a market for his coal? His coalfield was far, far from any
market. So, he would have to develop a market.

Porter was a most unusual man of exceptional talents. He was
born in Connecticut in 1850 and decided that his career would be in
mining. He attended the Columbia School of Mines in New York but
was dissatisfied with its training in metallurgy, which was the field
he wished to follow. Off he went to Germany and the Royal Acad-
emy of Mines. He completed his training in 1872 and headed for
Nevada where he became an assayer.

It was in 1875 that he decided to head for the San Juans and the
exciting mining developments that were attracting the nation's attention. In his travels he followed the Florida River into Colorado and
was amazed to see large coal deposits in either side of a narrow valley he traversed. Porter and his horse were laden with his clothes
and supplies, assaying equipment and two bags of coal which Porter
had carried all the way from Pueblo. He had heard nothing of a good
grade of coal existing in the San Juans and accordingly had brought
his own supply to conduct assaying. When he found himself virtually surrounded by coal beds of high quality, he emptied his bags and
went on his way to Silverton.

Meanwhile, up in Silverton, the Greene Brothers were having
trouble with their heavy investment in a smelting works. They seized
on Porter and put him in charge of rebuilding the Greene Smelter
and getting it into production. Most of the summer of 1875 was
spent in this effort which included the installation of a water jacket
for the furnace which Porter felt would do a better job than the previous brick and cement.

Porter (along with most of the town's population) left Silverton
to spend the winter in a warmer clime. But he was back in the summer of 1876 to put the up-graded smelter in operation. One of the
problems he faced was the low quality of the coal he was forced to

use. The coal came from Coal Bank Hill, the nearest source of any coal. It was miserable stuff. Despite the fuel problems, the reworked Greene Smelter turned out 140 tons of bullion worth $100,000. It was the only smelter in Silverton that was even partially successful.

But the problem of inferior coal plagued the smelter. The Greenes gave up and sold to the New York and San Juan Mining and Smelting Company in 1880, and Porter was kept on as superintendent.

Looking at his later dealing with railroads, it seems conceivable Porter may have negotiated with the D & R G to encourage them to speed their arrival to Durango and a year later to Silverton. Porter needed the railroad, because it furnished the first big market for his coal mines. There is no question that he had a close involvement with the railroad officials, because it was Porter, together with General Palmer and a Dr. Bell, who plotted out the Durango townsite, and Porter secured a hill for a site of the smelter which has ever since been called Smelter Hill.

The completion of the branch of the railroad to Silverton meant it could be used to carry Porter's coal to the Greene smelter, or the ore from Silverton mines could be carried to a new smelter in Durango. Porter determined on the latter course partially because it took more tons of coal to refine a ton of ore, and also because he could see Durango was a more central location which would attract ore from the other San Juan mining fields. So the Greene's smelter was torn down and rebuilt as a much more efficient one in Durango. The future of Durango was assured.

If Porter was to sell more coal, he needed to secure more ore to be sent to the Durango smelter. Porter looked to the amazing rich bodies of ore in the Red Mountains. As long as it had to be transported by wagon that ore might as easily be sent to Ouray as to Silverton. Otto Mears' plan for a railroad from Silverton to the Red Mountains would secure that ore for the Durango smelter. So Porter joined with Mears in building the Silverton Railroad to connect the Red Mountain mines with Silverton. Now the rich ores from the Guston, Robinson, Genesee and Yankee Girl would be carried to Silverton and Durango and treated there using Porter's coal, rather than going via Ouray to Pueblo for treatment.

Again, working with Mears, the Silverton Northern Railroad tapped the Animas Valley as far as Eureka, reaching rich mines in

Cunningham Gulch. Those ores were now carried down to Durango and treated at the smelter Porter managed and which used Porter's coal. New discoveries of rich mines at Rico and Telluride also caught Porter's attention. Otto Mears was already talking of constructing a railroad that would stretch from what is now Ridgway to Durango, tapping on its way the rich mines at Telluride and Rico. Porter didn't invest in this latest venture of Mears, but he certainly encouraged it. Seeing the possibilities from the Rio Grande Southern Railroad, as Mears was to name it, Porter went into action. He gathered another group of smelter men, and in 1890 the group bought the rich Smuggler Mine, high above Telluride in Ingram Basin. The price was that of a fire sale, $400,000, because in 1888 it was averaging a daily production only eighty tons with values of fifty dollars a ton.

The new owners of the Smuggler included James Grant of the Grant smelter near Denver, A. Eilers of the Pueblo smelter, and William A.J. Bell of the D R & G. With assurance of additional tons of ore from both Rico and Telluride, Porter added two new blast furnaces and two roasters to the Durango smelter. Of course this meant the consumption of more and more coal from Porter's mines. Porter was doing very well financially.

Porter and his associates could point to a Smuggler production of $10,000,000 by 1891, and the group capitalized on this. By 1900 another $10,000,000 was produced. In 1899 the Smuggler was sold by the group for $3,000,000. What a very nice profit!

In the meanwhile, Porter looked to other directions to increase production at the Durango smelter so he could increase his profits in coal sales. Ore from the mines centered around Ouray were being shipped via the D R & G to either Pueblo or Denver (and occasionally Leadville) for smelting. None was going over the Rio Grande Southern to Durango. So Porter entered the mining districts in Ouray.

Porter became interested in a new gold-bearing discovery which was to become the American Nettie. By the time of the Silver Panic of 1893, the American Nettie was one of the biggest gold producers of the San Juans. Its production kept the Ouray economy alive after the silver crash and until the Camp Bird Mine was developed and became a producer.

After the Silver Crash of 1893 a strange thing happened. With the closing of the silver producing mines the smelters came upon hard times also. But after a couple of years the smelters started encouraging the owners of silver mines to check them for gold. It wasn't long before the mines at Silver Lake (above Silverton) , the silver mines along Hanson Creek (above Lake City) and many of the great silver producers on the Red Mountains were in production again, this time mining gold! The old-timers used to tell me that the smelters knew of the gold in the ore they processed, but because the owners were only interested in silver, they neglected to tell these owners of the gold values and pocketed the gold ore for themselves. That is how the smelting barons became so filthy rich! That there was a smelting trust seems evident; we have seen how they worked together to buy the Smuggler.

Porter was deeply appreciated in his home town of Durango. If it wasn't for his smelter, there would not have been much of a town. He installed a streetcar line which never made money, but Porter uncomplainingly paid the deficit each year until its abandonment in 1920.

Nothing remains of the coal mining town Porter constructed up Wild Cat Gulch. The market for his coal virtually disappeared with the closing of his San Juan smelter. Nor are there rail tracks to his coal mines which were so important to the continuance of the Rio Grande Southern Railroad. Gone also is the Silverton Railroad. But both Ouray and Telluride should pay respect to Porter for keeping them alive with his producing gold mines following the Silver Crash of 1893.

The American Nettie Mine was one of the biggest gold producers in the San Juans in the 1890s. It was discovered just before the Silver Crash of 1893 and kept Ouray from becoming a ghost town. — COURTESY OF P. DAVID SMITH

CHAPTER 34

THE GRAVE BETWEEN TWO GRAVES

Louis King, carriage maker and stable owner, was one of Ouray's solid citizens. According to the manuscript written by Frank Rice on the "History of Ouray," King arrived in Ouray in 1877, but since his daughter Elizabeth was the first teacher in Ouray and taught forty-six students in 1876 — the first year of Ouray's incorporation — it seems probable that Rice slipped a year as to King's arrival. King had been born in Germany and came to Canada at age fourteen. There he married and had two daughters, but the death of his wife led him to seek new surroundings and opportunities, and he came to Ouray. Initially, he was most successful and built the Story building now occupied by the Ouray Variety Store. The construction took place just before the Silver Crash of 1893 which resulted in him losing the building to Judge Story who held the mortgage. Story's name promptly replaced King's on the building.

King married a second time in 1882 to a woman he had known in Canada before he came to Ouray. This marriage ended in a tragedy. Viola, thinking she was taking a dose of salts, took strychnine by mistake.

But it was his third marriage that deeply touched all of Ouray . He fell in love with the wife of a neighbor and good friend. Frances returned his love and divorced her husband to marry King in 1890. She soon became pregnant but decided her second marriage was a mistake, and determined to return to her first husband. While still King's wife, both she and the baby died while she was giving birth. King and Johnson were still good friends, but both wanted Frances to be buried in their own family plots in Cedar Cemetery. They compromised and bought a plot for Frances exactly half-way between the two. On the monument they erected, they inscribed "Our Frankie."

Frances' gravestone lies between her two husbands and is labeled "Our Frankie."
— AUTHOR'S PHOTO

CHAPTER 35

NEW CAREERS FOR SOILED MEN

William Munn came riding into Ouray in the early spring of 1876. He had come from Saquache, a considerable distance and which required him to cross the Continental Divide. It had been a hard trip, for the spring snows were wet and deep, and the only shelter to be found during that three day trip was at the Ute Indian Reservation. Like many making their way to the new mining camp of Ouray, he was young (thirty-one) and single.

Ouray was at that time less than a year old. Three rough log cabins were the only houses when that winter of 1875-76 got under-way; but a fourth cabin was built by all the men who stayed in Ouray that winter. This fourth cabin — which was two stories tall — was for "Mother Cline" the wife of Captain Cline, one of the founders of the new community. Munn set forth to build — or rather have built — the fifth cabin which was constructed on the site that is now occupied by the Citizens State Bank. It is probable that this cabin still stands and was moved two blocks further south on Third Avenue, as Main Street is officially named.

Willy, as he was still called when he died at age seventy-four in 1924, was the advance agent for the arrival of the rest of his family. It was his task to get a cabin built to house his father and stepmother as well as his younger brother Charles.

Charlie, as he was always called, was twenty-six. Both brothers were veterans of the Civil War. Since that war ended in 1865, eleven years earlier, they both must have been very young when they enlisted in the 101st Illinois Infantry. Ira Munn, the father, was sixty-seven, a tall and distinguished man. Mary, Ira's second wife, was young enough to have been the wife of one of his sons. She was a striking auburn-haired woman, thirty-three, and she quickly attracted the attention of the men of Ouray who were sadly short of female companionship. She was quite possibly the second or third woman to take up residence in the town.

Willy had a second assignment to accomplish before his family was to arrive. This was to secure an adequate piece of property to conduct the businesses in which they would soon engage. Willy accomplished his assignments and was waiting at the door of the new log cabin when the others arrived. The contingent brought several loaded wagons, one of which carried what would become Ouray's first sawmill. Quite obviously the Munns had come to stay and appeared with the necessary finances to make a big showing in the new camp.

When the San Juan County Commissioners incorporated the Town of Ouray on September 13, 1876, Ira Munn was appointed one of the five members of the Board of Trustees. Willy was appointed Town Clerk. Under the name of George Wilder & Company, the Munns bought eight blocks of property in the northwest area of Ouray. In his own name, Ira bought several building lots, including the one where the Citizens State Bank now stands. On one of those lots he also built one of the first frame houses in Ouray. After all, it was his sawmill.

The sawmill went into service almost immediately after Munns' arrival. It was because of this early arrival and operation of the Munns' sawmill that Ouray had relatively few log cabins and instead moved directly into the second phase of urbanization almost completely leaving out the first phase of log cabins.

The second most important need of a new mining community was the adequate sampling of ores to determine it they warranted the expense of shipment and treatment and to assure that the returns from mills and smelters were not shorted. The Munns soon brought the equipment for a sampling mill. Water was used for power and to assure sufficient pressure to power the equipment, the Munns dug a several block long culvert from higher up the Uncompahgre. Many years later after the sampling mill had ceased operating, boyhood friends and I were delighted to find a very large bootleg still in operation in that covered spillway which had been blocked off from the river.

While the sawmill and sampling works were operated under the name of George Wilder, there is little evidence that Wilder was anything but a silent partner, and that Ira directed operations. Wilder must have had some money invested, for the Munn boys were able to buy him out in ten years. The use of Wilder was really a subterfuge

by Ira to cover the fact that he did have assets, because Ira was officially bankrupt, and creditors, as well as the State of Illinois and the
federal government, were all looking for him.

Ira Munn and George L. Scott had been two of the most successful warehouse men and traders on the Chicago Board of Trade. As it
is today, Chicago in 1872 was the center of grain trading in the United
States, if not the world. Repeated scandals in trading resulted in the
Illinois legislature requiring that all grain warehouses be bonded and
licensed. Unfortunately the Great Chicago fire destroyed the records
and left behind a void of information.

It is against this background that Munn and Scott joined with others in an attempt to "corner" the wheat market. A "corner" is when a
commodity which is sold for delivery is so controlled by the purchaser
that the seller cannot make delivery except by buying from the purchaser. In layman's words all the available wheat had been secured in
the hands of a few who could then charge whatever price for the wheat
they wished." The attempt failed because of the great number of small
quantities of wheat held by farmers for feed and for seed. When the
value of wheat rose to artificially high prices, the farmers scurried
around and flooded the market with more and more wheat.

In an attempt to keep the market "cornered" the traders who were
involved had to borrow more and more money using the wheat they
had in their elevators as security. As they didn't actually have enough
wheat in storage to secure the necessary loans, they grossly misrep-
resented the amount of wheat that they actually did have. As the
wheat kept pouring in and into the market place, the price dropped
from $1.61 by $1.14 in a twenty-four hour period. The drop in prices
bankrupted a number of traders, and a subsequent investigation by
the state revealed the shortage in the amount of wheat they actually
held.

Ira Y. Munn was one of the most successful warehouse men in
Chicago. Munn had arrived from New Jersey in 1856 when he built
his first elevator. Munn became the president of the Chicago Board
of Trade at the beginning of the Civil War. Under his leadership the
Board of Trade actively supported the North, raised enough men for
three infantry regiments and an artillery battery and provided the
money to equip all four units. His two sons enlisted in the infantry
regiments. Until 1872 he was a much honored man.

The Munn Brothers' Sampling Works is in the background of this photograph taken in 1915 but the gentlemen in the foreground are an English investor and the manager of the Chrysophie Mine. — COURTESY OF P. DAVID SMITH

In that year, when his elevators were inspected, it was found Scott and Munn had installed false floors so that when grain was poured upon these floors it appeared the elevator had more grain than it actually held. The two sold out to Armour for ten dollars, and his agreement to cover all shortages of grain held against his receipts.

Ex-president Munn was expelled from the Board of Trade which ordered that wherever his name appeared on the records it was to be stricken. Munn became a nonperson in Chicago. Scott was arrested and released on bail, but Munn "fled the city before the marshal could find him."

When Ira Munn first set up business in Ouray he could not operate under his own name so he used the alias of Wilder & Co. Within three years he appeared before the Federal Court in Denver, and his bankruptcy cleared his debts.

Ira was injured in a fall from equipment he was repairing in the sampling plant. He lived for a short time before dying in 1882. His wife lived on for many years, keeping a home for her two stepsons. She lived in the frame house Ira built on Main Street which had been moved to Fourth Street , the second house south of the Courthouse. When the house was moved to make way for Beaver's Saloon (which became the bank) it was placed on the Fourth Street lot so the kitchen faced the street instead of the back of the lot as was usual in those Victorian days. Mrs. Munn liked it that way, for while she worked in her kitchen she could look out on the street and keep track of happenings.

The two boys, Willy and Charlie, spread out with their assay works, establishing assay offices in at least Rico and Telluride. They operated the sampling works until around World War I when mining in the San Juans took a disastrous tumble. The old sampling mill lived on as a ghost until World War II when it was pillaged for scrap. Today, there is no evidence of the mill which once served with the culvert of water from the river and with a special railroad spur.

I well remember the two Munn men when I was a boy. Every Memorial Day and Fourth of July, they donned their old shiney Civil War uniforms and rode as honored veterans in the first open touring car in the parade. Neither married, and as a boy I mistakenly assumed Mrs. Munn to be the wife of one of the brothers.

Ira died in 1882, Matilda (name according to cemetery records) in 1920, Willy in 1924 and Charley in 1928. All were highly honored and respected citizens. Ira, once a soiled man, found a respected career and a new life in the Colorado West.

CHAPTER 36

THE RIGHT WRIGHT BROTHERS

George and Ed Wright were pillars of society in early-day Ouray. Their wives were social leaders, active in the Ouray Women's Club, the Episcopalian church and in the Women's Christian Temperance Union. In fact, both wives at one time or another were the heads of the Ouray WCTU. George was an active civic leader and a very social man. Seemingly his only vice after getting married was to play cards with other community leaders in the saloon of the Beaumont Hotel — probably the most respectable of all the twenty or so Ouray purveyors of liquor.

What most of Ouray didn't know (and I doubt Mrs. Wright knew) was that George had held the first liquor license and ran the first legal saloon in all of the San Juans!

George Wright must be counted as one of the pioneers of the San Juans. The first migration to the rugged mountains came in 1860 when hundreds, if not thousands, followed the mysterious Charles Baker into the vastness of the San Juans. This was the first recorded adventure which ended in 1861 because of disappointing results from panning for gold and the breaking out of the Civil War. It wasn't until 1870 that three men again reached Baker's Park, and it wasn't until two years later that enough men spent a summer in the San Juans that they could hold a Fourth of July celebration.

It was in the winter of 1873-74 that George Wright (age twenty-eight) arrived at Del Norte, the "Gateway to the San Juans." At least we assume we have the "right" Wright, for there were no other Wrights known to be in the San Juans at that early time. Except for the earlier Baker Party, no one had yet spent a winter in the San Juans. The prospectors and miners in Baker's Park hurried out with the coming of heavy snow, and Del Norte was the favorite place to winter. They had a marvelous time in the winter, playing jokes on one another, and staging bawdy playlets. It was the kind of play George was sure to enjoy and quite likely be the leader of.

During that winter the Colorado Territorial Legislature designated a new county which covered all of southwest Colorado. It was called

LaPlata, and the legislature designated Howardsville as the county seat. But there was really no Howardsville — only a cabin built by George Howard, a pioneer of the failed Baker's Party and among the very first to return to Baker's Park. As the designated county seat the county commissioners needed a courthouse and contracted to rent a cabin nearing completion as long as the builder would construct a second one before winter arrived. A blacksmith set up his forge, another cabin was built for a store and still another for a bakery. Howardsville was becoming a true county seat. George saw an opportunity for gain and bought the two cabins housing the county clerk and the court. Shortly thereafter, he applied to the county commissioners for a saloon license and thus opened the first legal saloon in all the San Juans, if not on the entire Western Slope of Colorado. He soon had a rival in William Randall who also received a license. Randall was to become the first "resident" postmaster in Ouray just three years later. I say "resident postmaster," as there is no record that the first appointed postmaster actually ever set foot in Ouray. George was quickly assimilated into the community and found himself sitting on one of the first, if not the first, juries to serve in the new created La Plata County.

By the end of the summer, brother Ed had joined George. That same summer the new town of Silverton was founded, and in the fall an election was held which determined that there should be a new county seat. Most everyone left Baker's Park again for the winter. The very few that did stay the winter included the county clerk, Those folk who remained were the first to winter in the park.

The next spring it was obvious that Silverton would dominate over Howardsville and George sold his two Howardsville cabins and moved to Silverton. There he built two store-saloon structures, which according to Silverton's resident historian Allen Nossaman, still stand today. One was the Alhambra Saloon which George operated himself. Some accounts indicate he might have had a girl or two on the premises. Certainly he had gambling, for he was hauled into court, found guilty and paid a fine for gambling for operating the Alhambra. (That yellow front building has housed the "*Silverton Standard and Miner*" newspaper for many years.) Despite the court's slap on the wrist, George was doing very well.

Meanwhile Ed went in search of riches via prospecting. Along with W.H. Brookover, he went over mountain ridges and found himself somewhere near what was to become the town of Sneffles. There the two found evidence of good silver and staked the Wheel of Fortune Mine. Frank Hall, the father of recorded history of Colorado, relates "In the winter of 1875-76 George and Edward Wright came over (to the Sneffles Mining District) from Silverton on snowshoes and staked off the Wheel of Fortune Lode." However this information appeared in Volume IV of his history, for which he used less reliable sources and was written nearly twenty years after the fact. William Byers, who wrote in 1877, a date very close to the actual happening, says ". . .that the Wheel of Fortune was located October 7, 1875 by W. H. Brookover and E. Wright; subsequently G. L. Wright, Mason Greenlee and S.H. Crowell purchased interest."

Clearly Frank Hall was in error, for there are contemporary accounts of George going over Stony Pass to Del Norte to spend the winter of 1875-76. George might well have been on skis, but it was only to get over Stony Pass and away from the harsh San Juan winter. George did not spend the summer of 1876 at Wheel of Fortune, for he ran for sheriff of La Plata County and was defeated. However, he won a case in county court that year which was probably the first court case tried in La Plata county under the spanking new State of Colorado. (A new history of Ouray misinterprets Hall and the author concludes George and Ed snowshoed into Ouray, an obvious but understandable error.)

However George and Ed did spend winter days of other years working the Wheel of Fortune. They also spent long nights in isolation in their cabin at the mine. On one of these long evenings the two were reading a copy of "Heart and Hand". We might compare it today to a magazine of "True Confessions." It contained letters from writers seeking companionship, romance, and mates. George bet Ed $5.00 that he could interest one of the girls sooner than Ed could. And so the contest began, each writing to girls they selected from letters in "Heart and Hand."

George must have been the more persuasive. Soon he was carrying on a correspondence with a young lady from St. Louis. She informed him she was excited over her mail suitor and promised she would soon be on her way to marry George. This fun was turning into a serious problem. First, how could he tell what she looked like and what her temperament was. And second, and really important, the two men had just struck a six inch vein of ruby silver – a very rich strike that would make them both rich. Breach of promise to marry was in those days a very serious offense. If he refused to marry the lady almost any jury would make her wealthy and impoverish George.

What to do? In desperation, Ed wrote the lady that George had been caught horse stealing the previous evening and had been hanged. His last wish was that his remains be shipped to her. If she would send the money for the cost of shipping, he would gladly ship George to her. Need we add the disappointed lady was never heard from again.

The Wheel of Fortune was sold, and George's share was sufficient that when the 1880 Census of Ouray was taken he proclaimed that his occupation was that of "capitalist". Now being leaders of the town, George and Ed decided their next step was to get married.

First George rented a log house of two stories, and then he pursued a local school teacher. Lenora and George were married in 1879 at Leadville at her father's home. Because of the popularity of the young, fun-loving man, the young couple was met on their return by the Ouray brass band and escorted from the stage station across the Uncompahgre River to their new home. George did the expected, inviting all to come in and enjoy the new couple's hospitality. Probably that was the last occasion that the new Mrs. Wright permitted alcoholic drinks to be served in their home.

Lenore was on the serious side, while George was full of fun, jokes and was a "hardy good companion." Lenora was rigidly religious and opposed to gambling, drinking, betting and the nightly activities in Ouray's brothels. George enjoyed gambling, telling jokes, being the butt of newspaper stories, and of course he enjoyed a drink with his friends. While Lenora was in town, he considerately held his activities to low levels; but when she left to visit family and friends, the newspapers took pleasure in printing his escapades. Nevertheless, despite these differences, the couple lived amicably, and for their twenty-seventh anniversary renewed their wedding vows.

Ed also married, a month earlier than George, and like him married a serious bride. He almost immediately became involved in community leadership and invested his money in various Ouray developments. In 1881 he built Ouray's first two-story commercial building which still stands on the southwest corner of Main Street and Fifth Avenue. A few years later he added next to it "Wright's Hall", which all locals call the "Wright Opera House." After his death which resulted from pneumonia caught while working with his brother at the Grizzly Bear Mine, Letita assumed the operation of the Opera House. However, George eventually took over, paying her debts and taking ownership. Ed died in 1895; George in 1916. Letita had moved to Pueblo, but Lenora remained in her home until her death in 1938.

The Wrights are now only memories in Ouray. But what wonderful memories! In Silverton, they are all but forgotten.

One more story. George made an election bet with a friend named Felix Partin. The loser would have to carry a stove from a Main Street store to the winner's residence. Wright won the bet. Partin who was as large a man as George, swung the heavy stove upon his shoulders and started to go down to the Uncompahgre, to cross the river and struggle up the embankment to George's house. He had hardly left Main Street when the Ouray band (hired by George) marched out of the alley behind Main Street and started playing "Marching Through Georgia". Half the town turned out and accompanied the band and the struggling Felix to George's home where George had adequately prepared for the event, by opening a keg of beer and handing out doughnuts. Lenora was out of town visiting her father and had no immediate knowledge of the hilarious affair. But some "busy-body" sent a copy of the paper to her. She showed it to her father who was so angered he tried to convince Lenora to divorce George. George always said this was his narrowest escape, and he suffered in the doghouse for many a day!

George Wright: saloon keeper, gambler, mine owner, Opera House impresario, and capitalist! A man for all seasons. The right Wright for Ouray.

The Wright brothers were the discoverers of the Wheel of Fortune Mine which is shown here in 1877, just two years after the rich discovery.
— AUTHOR'S COLLECTION

CHAPTER 37 🌵

STORIES FROM AN OLD MINER

My memories don't go back to the days before Prohibition. After all I was born the year Colorado went dry. But Claude Miner, an old friend who was born in the house originally located on the lot where we later were to build our home, left me with some of his memories.

According to his recollections, there were thirty-five saloons and about one hundred girls in the red light district. A few of the girls were black and were in demand for "superstitious reasons." (I can remember a time men used to rub their hands over a black man's head for luck - I suppose there is some relationship between that and the old-timer's remembrances).

Every Ouray business block had at least one saloon, and there were five in one block. Gambling in the saloons was wide open: roulette, faro, 21, stud and draw poker and a few slot machines (I remember when we even had penny slots placed on the penny candy counters). Beer was $.25 for a two quart can. The bartender made a point of shooting the beer into the can hard so the foam would take nearly a quarter of the space. To outwit him, the boy sent after the beer would grease the inside of the can! Buying beer by the can was "rushing the can."

Drinks were $.15 for one, $.25 for two. The customer poured his own drink from the bottle; the bartender poured the chaser. At the dance halls a dance and a drink cost $.25 and a drink for the girl, $.15. The girls received a percentage for each drink and dance they sold; the ticket or check they received was deposited under the garter of their stockings - that was their purse. Of course hiking the skirt to place the check in the "bank" revealed the leg and the key to their room and was an incentive to attract the customer.

The girls were varied. Some very young, but most middle-aged. Some had a college education. There was a section of cribs in the back of the Chinese laundry near Rawley's barn that was occupied by Chinese. Some of the girls were Mexican, but most were of the same background as the miners of Ouray.

At the turn of the century Ouray's population was about 3,000 and another 2,000 miners lived in the "suburbs" — the bunkhouses and mining communities of Ash, Sneffles, Ironton, Red Mountain and Guston. With the large number of single men, the girls of the Red Light district were in great demand. While some were full-time residents of Ouray, many were on the "Circuit". The "Circuit" was a string of mining towns throughout Colorado, and the girls moved periodically from one town to another. At the end of two years the ladies had a vacation, spending several weeks in Glenwood Springs at the Hotel Colorado. This circulation of the girls provided a change of "stock" for their patrons, offering fresh faces and bodies.

The only time the saloons closed was on election day, and then it was only the front door. Access was easily available through the wine room in the back. The wine room was open to the ladies of the town as well as to the "girls" of Second Street. Women were not permitted in the saloons. One visiting lady in town saw the big sign "The Bank" and stopped in to cash a check. She hastily withdrew when she saw the cashier was wearing a white apron. "The Bank" was a saloon named for the faro bank.

The only alternative for entertainment for the miners other than the saloons and dance halls were with the fraternal orders. They provided a quieter surrounding, although almost all operated a bar and had card games. Ouray Elks Lodge still has two slot machines that date from the turn of the century. Besides the Elks, there were two Masonic orders, the Redmen, the Moose, the Odd Fellows, the Eagles, and the Owls. In addition to providing a haven of recreation, the various orders buried their members who were too often killed in mine accidents or died of pneumonia or "miners con" (the common name for today's silicosis) and had no one to bury them. Several orders had special sections in Cedar Hill Cemetery.

The saloons were very democratic. Many were respectable businesses in which the storekeeper, the barber, and the banker could be found "belly up to the bar" along with the miners.

Bottles were reused. Kids could get five cents for three small whiskey bottles, five cents for two medium bottles, and large ones brought five or ten cents each. Some of the girls saved the beer bottles from their customers and gave them to the kids for their salvage money. At the "Bird Cage," a popular house, there were cages of birds, and a boy could earn a few pennies by supplying worms, grasshoppers and other bugs. The girls also would use cut flowers to decorate their cribs; so boys often stole the flowers from various gardens.

The streets were lighted with arc light, the current passing through sticks of carbon. Once a week a rider aboard a horse would ride through town and unhitch the chain on each light pole which lowered and raised the arc light. The chain was fastened high on the pole so little boys could not play with them, but a rider performing this chore always wore cowboy gear including chaps and a ten gallon hat. After he lowered the arc light he would either trim the remaining carbon or else replace it with a new stick. The old sticks were in demand with children to mark sidewalks and walls.

Claude Miner, who shared these reminiscences, at one time spent a winter working at the Mountain Top Mine which was located at above 13,000 feet. He wrote that before spring everything was buried under snow. The boarding house was two stories, and by the middle of January the first floor was completely buried with access only through the second story. On the trail between the bunkhouse and mine was a light on a fifteen foot pole. By spring this light was only a foot or two above the snow. There was one shower for forty men, and a hard fast rule was the man wanting a shower was required to shovel enough snow into a tank to provide sufficient water for a shower. Most men didn't bother to shower. At the Tom Boy, with its hundreds of miners, there were only two bathtubs. It was necessary to get a permit from the office to use one. "Believe it or not, there was never much of a stampede for the bathtubs," Claude wrote.

Ironton got twenty or thirty feet of snow each winter. This buried most of the cabins, largely occupied by old-timers, until only the smoke stack was to be seen. Several lengths of stove pipe were stocked in the cabin and additional lengths added to the smoke stack as required. Miner served one winter as Ironton's postmaster, actually living in the post office. He wrote that the first thing he did in the morning was to check the smoke pipes sticking above the snow to make sure smoke was coming from each one and an old-timer hadn't died during the night.

I often wondered about the slots at floor level in all the outhouses. It seems that in the winter to go to the outhouse (and there

The Town of Ironton boasted a main street (which was really its only street of any stature) that was almost a mile long. — COURTESY OF P. DAVID SMITH

was no indoor plumbing) it was necessary to put on skis. The slots at the floor level were so a person could back into the small building without having to take the skis off or put them back on when leaving.

That story reminds me of the two families who lived not too far from us when I was a boy in Ouray. The families in two adjoining houses shared a common outhouse. We would often be awakened during the night by the ringing of a bell that each had at their back door. The occupant wanting to go to the outhouse would ring their bell and if no answer came from the outhouse knew it was clear to trudge through the snow to the crude facility.

CHAPTER 38

OUR FRIEND THE MURDERER

In our dining room, on the top of a marble covered table, is a charming small chest, lovingly made of hard woods. Open the lid and upon a cloth covered tray lies a myriad of sparkling crystal to greet your eyes. Some day in the future we will give the chest to the Ouray County Historical Museum; but not yet — it means too much to us.

The chest, 20 inches by 9 inches and 8 inches high, was painstakingly and lovingly made in prison by convicted murderer Billy Nagle. It was made for Marie Emerson, a young girl who became Billy's lifeline to the outside world in the years he spent at Canon City. For many years during her marriage the chest was a much loved showpiece in Marie's house. After her husband's death Marie moved to a retirement home where space was more precious than her former spacious house. Marie sent the chest to me to treasure and enjoy, but eventually it was to go to the museum; and it will.

Billy Nagle was a prospector and miner. In the winter of 1920-21 he lived in a cabin in Ironton. One night in February 1921 two others joined him for dinner and in working the still which was cooking on his stove. The three enjoyed frequently sampling the product as it "cooked". And that is the last thing that Billy remembered.

The next morning he failed to turn up at the nearby claim he was working. "Slim" Berry went looking for him and found him "passed out" in his bunk. Hiney Hall and Freddie Jacobs were lying on the bloody floor mortally shot. Nagle was arrested and brought to the Ouray County jail to be held for trial.

Billy denied any knowledge of what happened. He said the bottle had been passed around several times that evening. He remembered nothing more. He denied he had committed the murder but could point to no one else.

To those who knew the affable Billy Nagle, it seemed highly unlikely he could have committed a murder. Also living in Ironton at that time was a "ne'er-do-well", sometime miner, but more often he was a do-nothing. He had expressed a considerable desire for Billy's

The Sutton Mill and boarding house is shown in the foreground. The mine was across the canyon to the right. An aerial tram connected the two. — Author's collection

still. There was conjecture that he might have been the killer. . . . but suspicions don't amount to proof.

Judge Emerson, a distinguished attorney in Ouray, knew of Billy because the two came from the same Illinois town, although they were many years apart in age. Billy came from a respected family, and all of his activities since coming to Ouray were of the highest caliber. So the judge took an interest in the proceedings and obtained attorney Carl Sigfrid to defend Billy. Sigfrid had successfully handled other criminal cases.

The old brick county jail (which still stands next to the courthouse, although unused for jail purposes for many years) was Billy's address for a number of months while he awaited trial. Roy Laird was then sheriff, and according to custom, Mollie Laird, his wife, cooked meals, fed prisoners and was paid by the county for doing so. Mollie went on a vacation which meant Roy was now to prepare the prisoners' meals; a task he didn't relish.

Roy had an answer. Billy was a pretty good cook; in fact he had served as cook at one of the mines. Roy turned over to him the responsibilities of cooking and ordering the food. Roy also often turned the key to open Billy's cell and told him to go shopping. Billy did so, charging his purchases to the jail's accounts.

One afternoon Billy paid a social call on the Emersons. He joined the judge, Marie and her mother on the lawn, and they spent a pleasant afternoon. He explained to them, "They don't care, They leave the keys hanging where I can reach them." He begged Judge Emerson not to tell his family back home what had happened to him because they were highly respected, and he didn't want the family name blackened because of him.

In December (ten months after the shooting) the trial was held and Billy was found guilty and sentenced to fifteen to twenty years in the Cañon City prison. Marie frequently wrote to him, and he returned her correspondence. It seems she was the only correspondent he had during those prison years. He early on became a trusty and was paroled after only serving three or four years.

The Emerson's welcomed him home, and he was their guest for Christmas dinner. The judge was responsible for an old log cabin and offered Billy an opportunity to live in it in exchange for him making the cabin habitable. The cabin still stands in the alley between Fifth and Sixth Streets, next to the Portland Flume. In all probability it was the cabin where thirteen men spent the first winter in Ouray, had their famous Christmas dinner and drank their even more famous vinegar.

To go to the Presbyterian Church, my family passed the cabin. At first I was terrified of the "murderer" who lived there — after all I was only about seven. Big brother Frank was six years older, and he soon scratched up a friendship with the lonely man and spent some evenings with him listening to his stories of other years. Soon all four of us children were visiting with him. As Marie was almost an older sister to my sister Bernice, she followed Marie in accepting him. Nevertheless, as a jailbird there were many in town who looked askance at him. He became a lonely man.

Judge Emerson obtained a job for him as the watchman at the Sutton Mill which was located just south of Bear Creek Falls. He occupied a small shack on the other side of the Million Dollar Highway. The mill still stood until the 1980s when two hitch hikers sought shelter in the old mill, started a fire on the wooden floor and burned the picturesque old building to the ground.

Bill became more and more apprehensive and frequently answered the door with a pistol in his hand. Whether he feared a relative of the two murdered men would seek vengeance, or the loneliness of his dwelling was the cause of his apprehension, we will never know.

On a hot summer day he walked the four miles from the Sutton Mill to the Cascade Grocery, bought a few supplies and started his long walk back up the hills. It was now nineteen years and seven months since the night of the shooting in Ironton Park. Billy walked to the edge of town, sat down on a stone wall which edged Main Street, took his revolver from his pocket and killed himself.

Billy Nagle was a gentle man. He was kind to us children. He lived nineteen long and very painful years, which were surely sufficient punishment IF he did commit the murders.

We cherish the chest he so lovingly made for Marie Emerson. Someday it will be a fine exhibit in our museum. But not now — we are not ready to part with this treasure and the memories it holds in the velvet-lined interior.

CHAPTER 39

WINTER - THREE QUARTERS OF A CENTURY AGO

The knifing winter wind blowing from the snow-covered San Juans helps me to recall my much earlier San Juan winters. That wind sometimes whipped the wooden shingles from housetops, leaving an opening for trickles of melting snow to drip onto bedroom ceilings.

January weather, although we are now sheltered in well-insulated and centrally heated homes, recalls the magnificent "television" screen of yesteryears — the isinglass windows of the potbellied stove that held at bay the all-penetrating cold. Gazing into those isinglass windows we could picture the magical visions of the world we had never seen as they lay outside our mountain valley— skyscrapers, Florida beaches, knights and ladies, and dreams of the future.

The walls of the dining room where the stove was located were made of beaver-board - some sort of a pressed paper. Insulation in those walls consisted of sheets of newspaper which had no value as insulation but did serve as a barrier to keep the wind out. Throughout the rest of the house the walls were plaster, again with newspaper "insulation."

Around the middle of the potbellied stove wound a strip of chrome metal. The door handle was of chrome wire and the feet of the stove were covered with the same metal. From out of its top sprung a length of black stove pipe. An elbow turned the stove pipe in the direction of the chimney. We placed the stove at the other side of the room from the chimney so that more of its heat would be dissipated into the room before being expelled to the cold outside. Numerous wires looped the stovepipe and were fastened to the ceiling to keep the stove pipe from collapsing, falling to the floor and pouring soot all over the house.

The dining room was the center of our evenings. After we finished supper and washed dishes, it was here we gathered to study, read, play games and listen to stories. Light came from a single 40 watt light bulb that hung from the center of the ceiling, over the dining room table. The cord upon which it hung was wires covered with cloth. Occasionally a gust of wind would come down the chimney forcing smoke into our warm dining room.

The coal bucket stood beside the stove on our metal covered asbestos plate that protected the floor from the heat of the stove. It had been filled from the coal shed before dark came upon us and must be filled again before bedtime. As our father had died when I was very young this meant one of the boys would be selected for the unlucky job of leaving the warm fireside, putting on heavy overshoes and outer clothing, and plunging out the back door to run through the towering snowbanks that lined the way to the woodshed to fill up the scuttle and (at a much slower pace) trudge back to the house and the warm fireside. Thus coal and kindling would be ready to rebuild the fire in the morning. It made no difference how carefully the fire was banked each bedtime; by morning it had burned out and the house was bitterly cold. Without effective insulation the cold seeped and surged into our homes.

When bedtime came, we trooped into the kitchen where a brick was toasting for each of us in the oven of the cook range. The brick was gingerly retrieved from the oven, wrapped in flannel, and secured with a safety pin which would carefully be placed facing the foot of the bed. Otherwise that hot pin might result in a nasty burn if feet were accidentally placed against it.

In our family there were neither bedrooms nor beds enough to provide individually for each of us, and so we all occupied a bed with another member of the family. This lack of privacy was more than made up for by the increased intimacy of shared secrets and thoughts and the comfort of bundling to keep warm

Rising in the morning was a shivering experience. In that frigid room we gathered our clothes in our arms and raced down the stairs to dress in the kitchen beside the warm kitchen range. In addition to a pot of bubbling oatmeal and the great iron skillet that held the browning pancakes, the stove top also held the curling iron which would grasp my sister's hair to make it conform to the style of the day.

Dressing as a small boy was much more complicated than now. First came the long underwear with the buttoned seat. Then came a kind of vest with elastic hanging down to the legs which fastened the long brown stockings that came well above the knee (long stockings and short pants were the standard until graduation from the eighth grade; graduation brought the first pair of long pants!). Then came a shirt with buttons along the lower edge which was to be fastened to a pair of short pants; this button arrangement kept the pants from falling down around your knees.

Finally, there were the winter boots. When the snow was deep it was a matter of buckled galoshes. Clumsy and awkward, they must have given our teachers a really rough time. I remember how near the end of a class we started the process of dressing to go outdoors. There was a clothing area in the main hall for each room with hooks for clothing. When it got near to the time to go home we all went into the clothing closet or hall, sat on the floor and tried to get dressed. We had a sort of a snowsuit of heavy blue serge, that when finally it was donned must have made us look very much like teddy bears. When the snow wasn't too deep, we could wear our winter shoes or boots. I was particularly fond of a pair of Weatherbird boots that came from Vossler's store. One of the boots had a side pocket to carry a pocket knife. When I got the boots in the early fall I was without a knife and it became an important part of my Christmas list. I received the knife for Christmas and the next time I wore my boots to school, the knife was carried. Today having a knife in school would be against the Colorado law and result in a required expelling. Back then it caused no commotion or questioning.

In those days we had two schoolhouses. The grade school was located in the big stone and brick building and the high school in a yellow frame structure which stood east of the grade school. Snowballing was a particular joy for the boys of that day and the high schoolers threw their icy balls with a speed and force that both impressed and frightened us, the younger children. Snowball fights were strictly forbidden on the school grounds and at nearly every recess or noon hour one or more of us was marched to the principal's office to pay the penalty for having yielded to temptation. Paddling was an accepted discipline.

Most of us walked home for noon dinner, a few who lived too far ate lunch in a classroom monitored alternately by various teachers. Going home after school was a matter of getting into as much trouble as we could get away with. There were pits with hot water springs located near where the Weisbaden is now located and in the yard

This photograph of the GAR garage shows just how deep the snow can get in Ouray, although most of the time the winters are very pleasant. — AUTHOR'S COLLECTION

across the street. Often in mid-winter we would see garter snakes and frogs in the pit bottoms and, of course that required sliding down the muddy side to catch them and then thoroughly getting covered with mud in attempting to scramble back up again.

We all looked forward to after school and after supper sledding. As streets were not plowed, any street with a good hill was open for sledding. One hill we particularly used a lot had a full four block run down to the edge of the river and started with a particularly steep portion. Sledding was more fun when we piled on top of one another to increase the speed. The big bobsleds were particularly sought after. Most were homemade by fastening a board the length of two sleds with a pivot on the leading one. Other bobsleds were created in the blacksmith shops around town with strap metal coating the wooden runners. I remember a couple of stores bought bobsleds, but they were not common. As many as ten or twelve of us might squeeze on one of the sleds if we sat close, close together. This closeness was a great attraction for the teenagers, because hugging the one in front of you was necessary. These sleds traveled at a ferocious speed, crossed Main Street and finally plunged into an embankment that was a sort of dike at the river.

Motor vehicle traffic was not a problem, most autos and trucks were placed on blocks for the winter with their radiators drained and their batteries carried indoors. Only sidewalks were plowed, and the streets were left with snow until the spring melt. When winter arrived, the horse came into his own. Down at the Cascade Grocery the model T went up on blocks, and old Bessie, who had been enjoying a comfortable life in a pasture down the valley, returned to haul the delivery sleigh. No one carried groceries up the hills from Main Street, and every grocery and meat market delivered to homes. Main Street was plowed but not like today, and a good coating of snow was left for sleighs. Motor vehicles were not a problem for sledders. However, a misguided sled could crash into a fireplug with frightening results.

Winter was a time of bells. Nearly all of the teamsters and owners tacked bells on the harnesses. The ringing of the bells on the teams pulling the ore wagons filled the air in the evening as they came down from the hills to the barns. The huge ore wagons were converted to sleds by removing the wheels and replacing them with great wooden runners tipped with strap metal. When the teams arrived in town there were frequently icicles hanging from the noses of the teamsters, and the horses' faces were white with frost. I especially remember that the horses' long, ice-coated eyelashes were very striking. Mothers used to bring their daughters into the house when they heard the bells of the "sixes", since the language of the teamsters as they fought to control the contrary sliding sleds was most picturesque.

Bells, bells, bells. What a wonderful memory of the winter of our youth three quarters of a century ago.

CHAPTER 40

EQUALITY FOR WOMEN IN THE WEST

The West was largely regarded in history as a "Man's Country," and indeed in the frontier days men usually greatly outnumbered women. According to tradition the women who came to the West were, in general, highly regarded by the men and perhaps almost worshipped. In legend even the dance hall girl or those who made their living on a "hot mattress" were endowed with attributes superior to man and made super-heroic. So comes the story of little Silverheels who nursed the miners of Colorado's South Park through smallpox, contracted that scarring disease herself, and with her face ravaged and her means of livelihood ended, she disappeared from the mining camps. But she is remembered by the mountain named for her by the grateful miners.

Rarely, it would seem, were women the equal of men in the Golden West — they were superior! Only in a few recorded instances did they descend to the degenerate level of men. We think of Calamity Jane who sank to the equal level of men through drinking and carousing, yet she was still revered in a strange way.

There were even some women who descended to the level of lynching. One such case was Elizabeth Taylor of Nebraska, but better known was Cattle Kate of Wyoming who offered her services and that of her "girls" to the cattle hands in exchange for stolen cattle. This operation might have gone on indefinitely, (most ranchers in their beginning years had branded a few questionable mavericks) since cowhands would bring in a single steer to trade for services, but Kate became overly greedy and turned this simple retail trade business into a commercial wholesale one.

A lynching in Ouray, Colorado in 1884 was a different story and one far more depraved and unpleasant. This occurrence rocked the nation and resulted in wide editorial comment, some pro and most con. You be the judge.

During the night of January 23, 1884, the merchants, professional men, and other leading citizens gathered together, moved to the Delmonico Hotel where a Mr. and Mrs. Cuddigan were held, and overpowered the law officers who protected them. Then they escorted her and her husband to the Ouray city limits, hung him on the ridge of Tommy Andrew's cabin and strung his wife to the tree immediately opposite.

Perhaps the most definitive accounts of the lynching appeared in the *Solid Muldoon*, a weekly and sometimes daily newspaper published by David Day. The *Solid Muldoon* was easily one of the most colorful newspapers of the Western frontier. David Day, the editor, was engaged in a circulation battle with the more circumspect *Ouray Times* which provided him with even greater need to produce a more graphic publication than his extrovert nature normally required.

Origin of the name of the *Solid Muldoon* newspaper is somewhat obscure. There was a prize fighter with that nickname who had achieved some prominence in that day of bare-knuckle fist cuffs. But more probably the *Solid Muldoon* was named for a hoax that took place on the Front Range of the Colorado Rockies near Pueblo. There a stone giant was unearthed and amid fitting publicity was sold to Barnum for exhibition purposes. Of course the petrified giant turned out to be a phony, but it attracted wide publicity in the nation's press before the falsehood became evident. It was named the *Solid Muldoon*, in memory of the fighter who often looked like a solid stone on the floor of the boxing ring. Later that year Dave Day founded the newspaper with that same name.

There are few more colorful writers than David Day. Witness this item from January, 1884:

> The *Solid Muldoon* reports the receipt of a calendar from the Alton Railroad that featured an excellent and painfully attractive lithograph of Lillian Langtry. The British beauty appears clad in a low neck, short sleeve, put-your-hat-over- the-keyhole-harness that would have broken the original Adam all up and have precipitated David, the sweet tenor of Israel, to have blown himself in frequently and in great shape. *(Presumably the term "blown-in" refers to a mining term applicable to smelters and steel mills when the heated metal reaches such a molten stage it virtually explodes.)*

About a local businessman and non-advertiser. Day said: "He's the most even-tempered man in town — he's mad all the time."

When a prominent United States senator came to town to speak, Democrat Day proceeded to stretch out upon the ground. When the

Republican Senator standing out upon the back of an ore wagon asked with concern if Dave was tired, he replied, "No but I can lie here just as long as you can lie up there."

The first mention of the actions that caused the hanging was to appear in the editorial column of the *Solid Muldoon* for January 18, 1884:

> Lynch law, whether the atrocity of the crime justifies or not, invariably fractures communities into three classes, those who dare, those who dare not, and those who straddle the chasm between courage and fear and keep mum. The *Muldoon* claims to stand with those "who dare." And this prompts the assertion that we have a case of barbarity now in our midst that calls loudly and clearly for the rope. . . a case worse than cannibalism and without one extenuating plea or circumstance and one wherein an orphaned child of tender years has been tortured almost beyond the limits of human belief. The principal perpetrator being of the opposite sex has no weight with us, she herself is a mother which renders her actions doubly damnable, and entitles her to only such sympathy as the prudent husbandman metes out to the lamb-killing cur.

Further back in the newspaper appeared an account that had resulted in the editorial. The previous Sunday afternoon George Morrison, a school teacher at Dallas, arrived in Ouray and reported that he had stopped by the Cuddigan ranch and found that Mary Rose Mathews, an orphan sent out from the Catholic Orphan Asylum in Denver, had died that morning and had been buried in a mysterious manner. Morrison charged that the ten-year-old orphan had died as a result of barbarous and inhumane treatment.

The coroner went to the ranch the next day, exhumed the body and brought it to Ouray. A coroner's jury was selected on Tuesday, the body unclothed for a postmortem and after examination by Dr. Rowan and the jury, the doors were thrown open for the public to view the "damnable extent of the torture."

The article continued, "Think of it, a ten-year-old child, driven without food or raiment on bitter cold night to sleep in the straw stack. Not a square inch of the impoverished body was without cuts and bruises, her little feet frozen black and her fingers burnt and frozen to the second joint, her forehead marked and battered by cruelty and the base of her skull battered by a blow from one of the three wretches."

The jury findings were brief and simple: "Said Mary Rose Mathews came to her death from cruelty, mistreatment, and inattention at the hands of Mike Cuddigan, Margaret Cuddigan, his wife and James Carroll," and was signed by the six members of the jury.

Mary Rose's mother had died the previous summer, and her father, a Denver ex-policeman, had placed her with St. Vincent's Orphan Asylum until he could get work. The asylum reported Mary Rose to be "very bright and of extremely affectionate and loving disposition." The Catholic priest who was assigned to the Western Slope area, and served Ouray among many other communities, was to supervise her placement and report periodically to the asylum.

The Cuddigans lived on a subsistence ranch some ten or eleven miles north of Ouray in the Uncompahgre Park. They were relatively young, Cuddigan having married his wife only the year before while on a trip back to his home community on the Illinois River. Living with them was James Carroll, Mrs. Cuddigan's brother.

Following the exhuming of the body, the Cuddigans fled the area, but despite a severe snowstorm, the sheriff followed and arrested them before they could get away. They were then brought back to the county seat, Ouray.

At that time Ouray had no county jail, and the city "calaboose" (as the judge was later to refer to it) kept a determined person neither out nor in. So Cuddigan, his wife, and Carroll were confined to rooms in the Delmonico Hotel under guard by the sheriff and his deputies who were assisted by relatives who feared mob action.

Subsequently, witnesses were found who had visited the ranch for various purposes during the prior two months. They reported the child to be bruised, barefooted, and non-communicative. When they asked about Mary, the Cuddigans explained she had fallen into the cellar and bruised herself upon the cellar door. Subsequent investigation found a cellar but no cellar door.

Obviously the Ouray community was shocked. The ladies of the Catholic Church bathed the body with care and robed her with "tenderness it had never experienced in this lifetime" and conveyed the body to the city cemetery.

The editorial which suggested an appropriate lynching may have been an outgrowth of public feeling, or the public feeling may have been an outgrowth of the editorial. Ninety some years later this is difficult to determine, and more likely it was a bit of both.

On January 25, the *Solid Muldoon's* headlines screamed:

AVENGED!
By a Revengeful Populace!
ON THE MURDERERS
Of Mary Rose Mathews
rewarded with death by
VIGILANTES
Sheriff Rawle's Bullets faced
Without a Flinch by Men
Determined To Do
Or Die!

In an account which could only have been written by an eyewitness, David Day reported how the vigilantes, who were well and efficiently organized, quietly moved by side avenues to the Delmonico Hotel. Sheriff Rawles was overcome only after a fierce battle, and after he had fired shots in defense of the Cuddigans. His two deputies, Vanever and Woodcock, were "wilted by a brace of loaded Winchesters." Two brothers and a brother-in-law of the prisoners who were armed with "self-acting Smith and Wessons did not await a second order to go."

In a final statement, Cuddigan asserted his wife had been maltreating the child for a year before her death. This did not explain the evidence of rape and sexual mistreatment. The brother, Carroll, was

The Cuddigans were hung in a tree where the Ouray Hot Springs Park is now. The site would be just about where the "D" is in Detroit Photographic Co. in this photograph from 1890. — COURTESY OF P. DAVID SMITH

given a few hours to leave the county and availed himself of the opportunity. He was freed because he had been absent from the ranch the last few days of the girl's life.

The lynching then proceeded; the bodies being cut down by the coroner two hours later. Although Day made a major point of the supposed resistance of the sheriff, nowhere is there mention of the famed Ouray City Marshal Benton who was one of the most deadly and respected lawmen of the West. Obviously the affair was well orchestrated, and apparently most of the community was either in active or quiescent support.

David Day wrote extensively in later issues of the fine vigilante organization that existed in the town, of its sound organization and of the participation of the unarmed outstanding businessmen and community leaders. In fact Ouray had an enviable record of observance of the law. We have mentioned that no satisfactory jail existed, and further there is no record of a murder in the nine years of the town's existence. Doubtlessly this was in part due to the outstanding town marshal, which resulted in the difference between boomtown Ouray being obedient to the law, and the other mining boomtowns of Creede, Silverton, Telluride and Leadville having widespread gambling, crime and murders. The law breaker stood no chance against the guns of Ouray's marshal, and he knew it.

It was after the Cuddigan lynching that a controversy arose connected with the Catholic priest assigned to Ouray. The priest charged that the *Muldoon* was responsible for the lynching, and that the Cuddigans were innocent victims, the child having fallen and died from the resulting injuries. The priest's charges were widely published in Denver and even national newspapers which were already expressing shock and demanding that punishment be exacted upon the vigilantes.

Among the statements issued by the Catholic priest was that he had visited the child at the Cuddigan ranch at Christmas and found her to be in good health and happy. He had initially testified to St. Vincent's orphanage that the Cuddigans had an admirable reputation in Ouray.

The accounts of witnesses of the child's condition before Christmas begs the question. Had the priest actually visited the ranch and the child, or was this his concocted story to cover up the his negligence in watching over the child while she was in his area of responsibility and some 370 miles from the Denver institution? Certainly the Cuddigan's reputation was never one that was "admirable."

Further, the priest asserted that he had immediately come to Ouray upon learning of the death of his ward, that he had slept through the lynching party, and that had he awakened, that he would have defended the Cuddigans. Counter charges were made that he had indeed arrived the morning before the lynching, visited the Cuddigans at the Delmonico, had indicated the intention of staying at that hotel, but had without much persuasion accepted the suggestion he would be better off in the hotel across the street. It was questioned as to whether he could have slept through the gunshots and shouting that accompanied the lynching party which took place 150 feet from where he was sleeping. The infuriated townspeople suggested that if the priest dared to return he might be subject to the same treatment as the Cuddigans.

The priest did return a couple of weeks later to hold mass, which was attended by less than a dozen of the devoted miners and wives. (Ouray had a large southern Austrian-northern Italian Catholic population of miners and their families.) Because the priest reported he was present on the order of the bishop, he was permitted to remain. The bishop was assured the priest could come again on the bishop's business, but not on his own, and the bishop was asked to replace him. This eventually led to the establishment by the Little Sisters of the Poor of Ouray's first and only hospital. It was the same charitable group that operated St. Vincent's Orphanage in Denver.

The priest allegations plus the outrage expressed in many newspapers resulted in Governor J. B. Grant directing the body to be exhumed and moved to Denver for thorough examination. One result of this second and more professional examination was the finding that the child had been sexually abused and probably raped. A part of the account from the *Denver Tribune* of February 2 follows:

> A more impressive and pitiful sight has seldom if ever been witnessed in the country than that by the multitudes who flocked to the undertaking rooms of E. P. McGovern yesterday.
>
> At 7:00 A.M. the rooms of the establishment were thrown open, and over 100 persons were waiting to witness for themselves the fearful bruises and traces of atrocities and neglect that had been indulged by the rapist and murderers of the Cuddigan family.
>
> The poor little frozen feet and burned and frozen hands

attracted much attention while the scars of the lash and poker brought forth the bitterest denunciations. . .

Indeed it would have been the soulless brute who could have looked upon that inanimate child, victim as she was of scourge, rape and murder, without thinking harshly of her maltreaters, dead though they may be.

One woman remarked, "If the men of Ouray had not hanged the murderers, the women of the place should have turned out and taken the matter at hand!"

In the corners of the room and on the pavement assembled little groups of men, not idle, worthless fellows, but business men, who had taken the time to investigate and judge for themselves the correctness of the assertion of the daily press. . . .they universally conceded the conduct of the business men of Ouray was imminently proper. . .

Not one was heard to condemn the vigilante committee of Ouray and not a single word was uttered in defense of the lynched parties.

Following the Denver investigation and public exhibition, services were held in the Catholic Cathedral, attended by upwards of 25,000 persons, the remains were taken to the cemetery and buried alongside her mother. The people of Ouray paid for the expense.

The Ouray Catholics petitioned for the removal of the assigned priest. And the *Muldoon* intoned: "It is the responsibility of a community to protect its children. This we have done. If Denver had done as well, Ouray would not have needed to."

Subsequently the District Judge came to Ouray and assembled a Grand Jury. His first charge to the jurors was to investigate the need for an adequate county jail. His last charge dealt with finding the persons guilty of conducting the lynching. Here were the findings of the jury:

> That as to the special matters given in charge relative to the lynching which occurred in Ouray in January of the present year: They by leave do state that diligent inquiry has been made and owing to the fact that those parties, who, from the nature of circumstances are able to give most reliable and definite information, to wit: the officers in charge of the prisoners, they being unable to give any clue before our body at the present service, no action has been taken.

Thus closed the lynching of Margaret Cuddigan. It does not close the question as whether a lynching is ever justified.

CHAPTER 41

THE TRUE STORY OF FINDING THE CAMP BIRD?

The story of the finding and development of the fabulous Camp Bird Mine is generally repeated from the speech Tom Walsh made at the Colorado School of Mines some years following the discovery. It does seem quite logical to accept Walsh's words – after all he was the owner and proclaimed discoverer. But there is more to the story than that related by Tom Walsh. There is the story of three very different men. One a prospector, one a stableman and the third a dump grabber.

First there is the story told by Walsh. He had purchased a smelter in Silverton. It wasn't a very good smelter, but it was Walsh's. According to the repeatedly told story, Walsh needed siliceous ores to add as a flux to the ore he was treating from Red Mountain's Guston Mine. His need for such ores required him to lease various mines in the Silverton and Red Mountain areas, but it was necessary that such mines also have other ore values or their operations could not pay. As there was no such rock available in the immediate Silverton area, he contacted Andy Richardson to look for the ore in Imogene Basin which was located on a tributary of the Uncompahgre.

The Martha Rose Smelter which Walsh purchased in 1890 had been constructed in 1881-82. It had been the victim of lack of capital and many legal entanglements. The most lucid account of the Martha Rose is carried in Allen Nossaman's Volume III of "Many More Mountains" which also carries a photograph of the Martha Rose, which reveals it to be a most respectable smelter. However the smelter worked only three days after "blowing in" in 1882, before lack of capital closed it down, so the smelter never played a significant role in the development of Silverton. Walsh did make it work in 1890 by installing new smelter equipment, and the Martha Rose continued to operate until 1897. By then Walsh's attention was drawn to Ouray's Imogene Basin, and the smelter fell again into disuse. The last remains of the smelter were bulldozed away only a decade ago. The man Walsh supposedly sought to locate the siliceous ore body was Andrew W. Richardson. By the time I knew Andy Richardson he had fallen on hard times, and he seemed to me to simply be one of those broken-down miners who sat on the benches in front of stores on Ouray's Main Street. My father regarded him highly and we were instructed to treat him with respect.

Andy Richardson was born in 1853, and he was only eighteen when he came with his partner Billy Quinn to the San Juans in 1871. At that time the San Juan Mountains were still owned by the Utes, and they were among the first white men to enter the legendary mountains following the Civil War. The two prospected widely and successfully. In 1872 they staked out the Shenandoah, a claim of some significance which was located at the head of Cunningham Gulch. The same year Richardson took part in the Fourth of July celebration held in Arrasta Gulch. Arrasta Gulch was the location of the Little Giant, the first successful mine that brought mining men tumbling into the high Animas River Valley. Richarson and Quinn lashed a gun to a log intending to repeatedly fire it while the orator of the day was reading the Declaration of Independence. But the third time the overloaded gun went off, it exploded with one of the flying parts very nearly decapitating the speaker. Boys would be boys and after all Richardson was only nineteen. By 1874, Richardson and Quinn had located the Highland Mary which was to become one of the most storied mines in the Animas country. Initial assays ran as high as $2,244 of silver per ton! With no money for developing or installing milling equipment, the locators sold the mine to Edward Innis. Innis reportedly paid $50,000 to a New York medium to tell him where to dig in the mine.

In the summer of 1875 Richardson went prospecting in new country and crossed over the mountains into a hitherto unprospected valley. He was struck by the beauty of its tumbling waterfalls and masses of flowers and named it Imogene, because it was as lovely as the girl he hoped to marry some day. He and Quinn spent the winter, probably with the finders of the Wheel of Fortune, in what was called Richardson's Camp for many years. Richarson's Camp was located only slightly east of what was to become the community of Sneffles and was eventually swallowed by the Sneffles settlement. As Jack Benham points out in his "Camp Bird and Revenue," Richardson's camp became the first white settlement in the Uncompahgre-Gunnison drainage since 1828 when Antoine Robidoux built the short-lived Fort Uncompahgre near present Delta. Richardson and Quinn discovered and sold many claims, among them the site of what later became the Gertrude Mine.

The following year, 1876, Richardson tarried too long in Imogene Basin. Caught in a furious early winter snow storm, he and a companion set out to cross over the range to Silverton. Their two horses froze to death in the blizzard, and the two men had to fight their way through towering snow drifts without the use of snowshoes. By the time they reached Silverton, Richardson's feet had frozen so severely he was unable to get his boots off for three days. When he did recover sufficiently he headed to the outside world and married his beloved Imogene.

For the first several years of their marriage they lived in Richardson's Camp. The lovely Imogene was generous in her care of the prospectors who lived in nearby cabins and shacks throughout Imogene, Yankee Boy, and Governor Basins. They often enjoyed a hot meal and a touch of home at her table and shared Thanksgiving and Christmas feasts with the Richardsons. In appreciation, one Christmas, the miners, teamsters and prospectors gathered money to buy her a lovely fur coat — much the finest of any in the San Juans. In later years Andy moved Imogene to town and bought the home at 401 Sixth Street that is now occupied and rebuilt by the Robert Stouffers. We later lived next door in the two-story Victorian home that formerly had been rented to Tom Walsh to house his family while he was developing the Camp Bird. We assume Walsh rented the house because it was next to Richardson's.

Andy and Imogene were not to be blessed with children, so they adopted a nephew, Guy. Imogene died in 1908 after a long illness. Her tombstone recorded her birth as 1851, although the newspaper obituary listed her birth as 1859, which would make her age forty-nine at her death and Andy age fifty-five, which seemed more likely. Andy seemed to have lost his ambition with the death of his lovely Imogene. He later moved to Montana to live with Guy, and there he died in 1932. Andy was a founder of the Ouray Masonic Lodge, and his Masonic brothers brought his body back to Ouray and buried him in Cedar Hill Cemetery next to his beloved Imogene and erected a small tombstone.

But to return to Tom Walsh and his story of finding the Camp Bird. Andy Richardson has left a quite different story than that told by Walsh. It seems that Walsh was interested in the possibilities of Imogene Basin for mining and not necessarily just to locate siliceous ores to use in his Martha Rose smelter. It is now time to bring a stableman into the picture.

The year was 1894 and the Silver Demonization of 1893 had collapsed much of the mining in the "Silvery San Juans." John Ashenfelter had hundreds of horses, mules and burros that were no longer hauling ore from the now closed mines; nor of course was he hauling supplies to them. But the animals had to be fed. So Ashenfleter turned to mining in Imogene Basin.

John Ashenfelter was born in 1853 in Pennsylvania. By the time he was twenty he was a teamster hauling supplies to settlers doing business at the military forts scattered across the Great Plains. He caught the eye of A.E. Reynolds, who had several Indian trading posts, including the posts at Fort Lyons, Colorado; Camp Supply, Kansas and Fort Elliott in the Texas Panhandle. To supply his trading posts Reynolds went into the freighting business and soon had contracts with the government to provide various military installations. As Reynolds' activities broadened, he depended more and more upon his young teamster John Ashenfelter to take over the management of his wide flung freighting business. Reynolds began to supply the mines of Colorado, and this led him to the purchase of the Virginius Mine.

Located at an extremely high elevation of 12,600 feet, the Virginius had only a rocky, treacherous trail for access. Reynolds needed assured transportation to carry his rich Virginius ore down to mills and smelters. He called upon John Ashenfelter, who invested in a few burros and was soon packing supplies to the Virginius. When a rough wagon road was scratched out as far as Richardson's camp, Ashenfelter bought wagons pulled by six mule teams and at that point transferred ore from the pack saddles of the burros to the more efficient ore wagons. It wasn't many years before the Ashenfelter teams and mule and burro trains were hauling ore from the Yankee Boy, Humbolt, Sidney and other prosperous mines from what we call today the Sneffels area. At one time Ashenfelter was reported to have thirty wagons with six-horse teams, and 150 pack mules and burros engaged with an additional fifty horses for rental. In 1893 the Silver Crash left him with only a reduced volume of ore to be carried from the Virginius and none from the other big properties which had closed down. Thus, it was that Ashenfelter was seeking a way to feed and keep his stock.

Ashenfelter came up with a scheme to put his stock to work hauling supplies and ore. Both he and Richardson were working on properties in the Imogene Basin. From the writings of Warren C. Prosser (well-known and highly respected engineer and mineral surveyor) who interviewed Richardson came the following story:

> Andy Richardson and John Ashenfelter were working on various claims in Imogene Basin. Walsh was considered a "dump grabber" by both of these men. That is, he would take a property, work it out, shoot it in and then go off and leave it.
>
> One day John Ashenfelter said to Andy: "Tom Walsh is coming up to look at the Hidden Treasure claim." (Note: The Hidden Treasure was located in 1878 and by 1894 it had been developed with 500 feet of workings on two levels.) "You let on you have a lease on it and get him to take it. I've got a bunch of stock (mules and horses) eating their heads off doing nothing and if Walsh takes the Hidden Treasure it will give me something to do."
>
> Walsh came up and put the proposition to Andy that he turn the lease and option over to him, but that he would want to modify the terms. Andy listened to his "bull" although he called it a softer name.
>
> Finally Walsh asked Andy if this talk interested him. Andy replied, "No, I don't see where I'm going to come in on it." Walsh then stated that he would compensate Andy with a position, at which Andy got real mad saying that he had never worked for anybody in his life. He then turned to Walsh and said "I haven't got a lease on the Hidden Treasure, but I can get it. If you want it I'll turn it over to you and you can go on your own responsibility."
>
> Walsh then wanted to know where Andy would come in and Andy said. "Well, my object in getting you to take it is because I own the next property and you'll have to buy that. You can't go more than 500 feet on Hidden Treasure ground."
>
> Walsh then wanted to know what Andy wanted for his claim and Andy said, "When you want it we'll talk business."
>
> Walsh then got busy and got a lease on the Hidden Treasure

and its old mill. He then came up and said to Andy, "I suppose you know I've got the United States Mill." (The U.S. Depositor Mine was located by H.E. Wright in 1875 and had been developed with a mill built to handle the ore; it had ceased operation some years before).

Andy said, "Yes."

"Well," Walsh said, "How much do you want for your claim?"

Andy said, "I told him a price that I thought would stagger him, but he says he'll take it." At that time I was also working on the connecting claim in the bottom of the gulch and I had run a tunnel seventy five feet to get into my vein to make a discovery. So Walsh says to me "what will you take for the claim you are working on now?" I told him and he said, "I'll take it too." "Now," he says, "I can't pay you all cash, but I'll give $1,000 cash and the balance as I can, but when you get done with your work I want you to work for me." I finished my work and thought Walsh was all hot air, so I decided to go to town (Ouray). So I packed my burro and started down past the United States Mill and Walsh caught me. He asked me where I was going "I says to town." He says, "But I thought you were going to work for me, aren't you through up here yet?" I said, "I am." "Well," he says, "when will you be ready to work for me?" I said, "Right now." So he outlined his plan and we got busy on several properties. Along about spring, he said he wanted to get a sample for the Gertrude. He asked me several times if I had been over to it, so one day I did go over and go in and I took down some of the ore and got about half a sack full. It was fine stuff.

When Walsh started down the next day he asked me if I had been over to the Gertrude yet and I said "Yes." He asked where the samples were and I went and got them. He said, "Dump them out on the ground." I did so and he looked them over without getting off his horse. "I'll go over to the gorge and look at in the morning," he says.

Next day came and we went over to the gorge where I had got the samples from. He got in it and commenced to break rock. "Hmmmmm," he says, "It doesn't seem possible it can lay in here like this." He broke pieces, looked at them again and put them in his pockets. "Give me your gloves," he says. Then he broke some more until he had his pockets filled. Then he commenced to hand the stuff to me. He sent these samples to Ouray and Silverton to be assayed. They assayed out to have between 1500 and 1800 ounces of gold to the ton.

Andy Richardson says his profit in locating what was to become the Camp Bird was $10,000. Tom Walsh would produce four million dollars worth of ore out of the Camp Bird within the next six years and later sell the mine for five million.

Note: Andy had staked out the adjoining claim to the Gertrude which he never sold to Walsh, and it earned him a tidy profit as the Camp Bird developed. It was later sold along with the other Camp Bird holdings to British interests. Andy was the superintendent of the Camp Bird up until its sale to the British.

And so it was that the stableman, the prospector and the "dump grabber" all benefited greatly from the Camp Bird Mine. The stablemen, because he had to replace the mules used to pull ore wagons with the great horses that so characterized early Ouray, and he added many more teams to his operation; the prospector because of his small holdings which became very valuable and his position as superintendent of a great mine; and the "dump grabber" — well he just made millions and millions.

So which story is the correct one on the finding of the Camp Bird Mine? Walsh's or Richardson's? Or do the two stories need to be blended together?

This early-day postcard shows the workings of the Upper Camp Bird mine — the spot where Tom Walsh struck it rich regardless of whose version of the story is told.
— Author's collection

CHAPTER 42

THE YEAR SANTA ALMOST DIDN'T COME

It was one of those real honest-to-goodness winters that hasn't happened in recent years. Yet this winter wasn't so very far back, only in the early 1980s. The local miners who were trying to get over Red Mountain to work in the Sunnyside Mine faced deep drifts and kept wary eyes upward toward the steep slopes from where the snowslides plunged. The highway crews worked ever so hard and faithfully to keep roads open for the miners. In Silverton, men were shoveling snow off roofs to keep them from collapsing, and the piles of snow from the roofs made even greater problems for the embattled crew trying to keep Greene Street open. Already the city crew had piled snow high into the center of the street. The piles were so high that they eventually collapsed outward into the lanes on each side that they were fighting to keep clear.

In Ouray, snow was plowed to each side of the street, and the traffic on Main Street was confined to two narrow lanes. In the residential areas the snow at intersections was piled so high it was impossible to see an approaching car until it hesitantly poked its nose beyond the snowdrifts.

Down at Rice Lumber Company the edge of the slanting roof which normally was about eight feet off the ground was now actually hidden by the depth of the snow which piled from slides that shot down the roof in a futile attempt to reach street level. It looked remarkably possible to walk directly from the snow level on the street up the roof of Rice Lumber. Oh yes, this was truly a San Juan winter of the kind legends are made!

It was the middle of December, a night when the moon's rays glanced over the snow-capped houses of the town, with the only sign of life coming from the smoke of a few chimneys that drifted upward. Christmas was a week away and the scene of the snowbound little town couldn't help but remind an observer — if there had been one — of "The Night Before Christmas." But this wasn't Christmas Eve.

The Rice Lumber Co. has been operating in Ouray for over a hundred years. This image of the lumber yard (in the clearing) was taken about 1930. — COURTESY OF P. DAVID SMITH

It wasn't Christmas Eve, but what was that great deer with huge antlers doing on the roof of the lumberyard? It appeared he was investigating something as he walked across the roof top, when suddenly with a crash he disappeared. He had stepped upon a skylight, the glass had broken, and he had tumbled through to the floor inside the store.

While it was quite a tumble the big buck was strong and rose to his feet without difficulty. He wandered around the interior, his great antlers knocking brass doorknobs here and there, and a lot of other hardware went tumbling. All the doors to the outside were closed and locked, so he could not get outdoors. But things weren't too bad, the big fellow discovered a pile of bags of bird food. This made a delicious meal for the deer, and of course it was warm inside. With a comfortably-filled stomach he lay down and napped!

When morning came he was awakened by the proprietor coming to open for the day's business. Imagine the surprise of the owner when he opened the door to find himself nose to nose with a most unhappy buck with its head lowered and antlers at attack position. Fortunately, the man stepped quickly aside and let the deer have the right of way. Funny thing, by the time the proprietor recovered from his surprise, the deer had vanished and his tracks led only a few yards from the door before they disappeared too. It was the children of Ouray that soon were able to explain the strange happenings on the week before Christmas.

Sometimes when the weather conditions are most unusual, Santa takes special precautions. We all know the story of Rudolf and how he was called upon to lead the sleigh when the weather was cloudy and foggy. This year with the snow so heavy on housetops in the San Juans, Santa wanted to check the rooftops to be sure when his sleigh landed it wouldn't go through the roofs. So Santa sent out one of his most trusted reindeer to check Ouray's rooftops before Christmas Eve. The snow was so deep in the San Juans, his reindeer agent was unable to distinguish that Rice's Lumber Company headquarters was a store rather than a home, and so he had touched down, only to come crashing through the snow covered skylight.

As the children learned, the very angry reindeer, returned to the North Pole, and informed Santa the he had been sorely mistreated "by those rough miners that live in Ouray." He urged Santa to omit Ouray from Santa's Christmas Eve journey. If Santa did this, there would be no Christmas that year in Ouray and perhaps nowhere in the San Juans.

Happily, Santa disregarded his agent's advice. Santa arrived on schedule with plenty of presents in his sleigh, and the children received sleds, dolls, balls and all sorts of presents!

CHAPTER 43

A LOVE STORY

The Miller family came from Switzerland, arriving in the San Juans shortly before the turn of the century — sometime in the mid-1880s. They were not well educated but were known for their warm hearts. They settled first in the mountain community of Mineral Point. Somehow they managed to live in their two-room cabin all year 'round for several years. During at least two years they were the only winter residents in that tiny community. It was during one such winter that Mrs. Miller gave birth to her first of five children — all alone with only her husband to assist her.

Eventually the family moved from Mineral Point to the even smaller mountain community of Poughkeepsie, which was located hundreds of feet lower than Mineral Point but was still snowbound each winter. At various times there were two mining communities called Poughkeepsie. The earlier one was at the head of Poughkeepsie Gulch at about 12,500 feet. The Millers located in the latter Poughkeepsie which was located at the foot of the gulch where Mr. Miller worked in the Alaska Mine, which in earlier years had been owned by Horace Tabor. But his major employment was at the Old Lout Mine and there also Mrs. Miller became the cook.

Snowslides in the gulch were fearful, and the Old Lout Mine only attempted to operate all winter on a couple of occasions. The mill was taken out by slides at least twice, the last time signaling the end of mining operations for many years. At sometime during those years of working for the Old Lout, the family began to move into the town for the winter. One year they spent in Silverton, but usually the winter was spent in Ouray. It was there that the five children received very limited schooling – since the family arrived late in the fall (a month or so after school started) and left early in the spring before the school closed for the summer.

Then there was the matter of economic necessity. All the boys had to leave school and go to work when they were of high school age. One became a mule skinner, a second went into the mines, and the third became a cowpuncher. It is this cowpuncher, Ernest A. Miller, who is the object of this love story.

Ernest Miller began riding the range for a Cow Creek ranch at age sixteen. He later told me that he read cowboys received thirty dollars a month at that time. He said he was paid only twenty dollars and never was able to afford even a good pair of cowboy boots. Life on that Cow Creek ranch was tough, and the two or three years he spent there were not pleasant.

Then he learned of an opening at the Highland Ranch, owned by Axel Erickson and his wife Agnes. The Highland Ranch was located about four miles north of Ouray, up Forsman Creek which was named for the pioneer rancher who homesteaded those mountain meadows at a time when the Ute Indians still occupied the valley below. Forsman was the father of Agnes Erickson.

The Highland Ranch was perched high above the Uncompahgre Valley with its only access either by the Dallas Trail or a miserable road that had been scratched out along the red cliffs on the west side of the valley. At the time of which we are speaking, the deep, narrow road might have better been called a mountain trail. As the years passed, attempts were made to improve it, but it wasn't until the coming of the bulldozer that any marked change took place. In fact years later in 1936 while driving down that terrible scratch in the cliffs, Axel's truck slipped out of gear, the truck jumped over a precipice, and Agnes was killed. It is understandable, therefore, that in those early years of the twentieth century that Agnes found it advisable to leave the ranch when the school year began and set up housekeeping with her two daughters in Ouray to assure that they might go to school. Axel, with a ranch hand, was left behind to operate the ranch.

My earliest memories of the Highland Ranch and the Erickson family go back to 1920. We had been invited to have Sunday dinner with the Ericksons. Father went to Raleigh's stable (the old red painted building still standing at Main Street and Ninth Avenue in Ouray) and rented a two seated surrey. It was drawn by two horses, one of which had a colt which ran alongside, and that kept my interest during the long trip. On this conveyance we rode in style through town with my father tipping his hat gallantly to all the ladies and cocking his whip at the men. I particularly remember a mother burro we passed down near the American Nettie Mill; what made this burro memorable was that she had a pure white colt — the only solid white burro I ever saw.

At the ranch we had a fine meal and listened to the two daughters in a short concert. We then went out to view the ranch workings. I was particularly impressed by the barn which was built into the hillside so that both floors had access to the outside without having to climb stairs. This was also my first occasion to meet the two Erickson daughters, and I was much taken by Ruth who must have been all of eighteen-years-old.

It was with the Ericksons that Ernest first found himself living a true family life, since his childhood had been one of bare existence. Now, although only a cowboy, he was taken into the household in a warm and commodious log ranch home reflecting love and a culture that was entirely new to him. The Highland Ranch home was filled with fine furnishings and surrounded by lovely gardens. The ladies of the Presbyterian Church looked forward to their annual social meeting held at the ranch with bowers of roses decorating the room and music played on piano and viola by the two girls.

The Erickson's had two daughters. Charlotte was the younger and Ruth several years older. Charlotte played the piano, Ruth the viola. In the evenings the young cowboy sat with the family while Agnes read aloud from the works of James Fenimore Cooper and Mark Twain, or the two girls played music. Both the stories and the music were new to Ernest. Perhaps it was inevitable that Ernest and Ruth were soon attracted to one another. But Ruth was in her early teens and Ernest was nearly twenty. Ruth was also already showing signs of becoming an accomplished musician. Ernest was only a rough, barely educated cowboy.

The decision was made that Ruth, accompanied by Agnes, would go away to take music lessons and go to school. Certainly there was no instruction available in the San Juans that could provide the kind of music education Ruth should have. But Ernest didn't kid himself, he knew the departure of Ruth was to assure space between Ruth and him. Ernest realized that he wasn't "good enough" for the charming and talented Ruth, but he was determined to become "good enough," and he saved ample money that he could go to a business school. Then he came back to Ouray and obtained a position as teller at the

Citizens State Bank. Ruth finished high school, and then graduated from Western State Teachers College in Gunnison. She taught school in Eckert, and later while working in Gunnison she met her first husband who was the youngest United States Forest Service supervisor in the country. They subsequently lived in many parts of the country ranging from the Black Hills of South Dakota to Washington D.C.. Theodore K. Krueger was highly respected and rose to high positions with the Forest Service. Eventually the couple retired to Lakewood, Colorado, built a lovely country home, and there "T.K." died of a heart attack.

During her many happy years with T. K., Ruth had continued with her music and played with many chamber groups as well as the Denver Symphony for twenty-one years and the Mesa Symphony for a shorter period. Her daughter, Ruthabeth, became an accomplished musician also, and by the time she was sixteen was nationally recognized for her violin expertise.

Axel Erickson saw great possibilities in the cowpuncher he had brought to Highland Ranch, and he persuaded Ernest to attend the University of Denver College of Business. However his career in the Citizens State Bank became limited by the Great Depression. Ralph Boyd was the cashier and nominal head of the bank. Ralph Kullerstrand and Ernest were two bright young men on the way up and both invested in the bank's stock. With the onset of the depression it became obvious that the bank did not need, nor could it afford, to keep both young men. Ernest sold his stock to Ralph and left Ouray to go to Denver where he secured a position as a teller with the International Trust Co. He was a treasured employee. The International didn't have a retirement program for its employees, but when it came time for Miller to retire the officers voted a special pension for him.

The years that followed his leaving Ouray were hard ones for Ernest. He wrapped himself in dreams of creating a great mining company that would be centered around the Poughkeepsie country that he knew as a youth. He carefully saved and bought up mining claims for their delinquent taxes. He paid San Juan County to cut a road from the beginning of the Poughkeepsie Gulch up to Lake Como—the very road jeepers use today. Thus when his hoped for mining operations were begun he would have truck access to the Old

This was the white burro that the author saw on his way to the Erickson's Ranch. It was a rare sight - the only white burro the author has ever seen. — AUTHOR'S FAMILY COLLECTION

Lout, the Amador, the Saxon and the many other mining properties which he had accumulated.

He eventually moved into our home and became a part of our family. My father had died when I was just five, and Ernest became a combination older brother and father image to me. Then came my graduation from the University of Denver, a job in Washington, and the long war years in the Air Corps. For the next fifteen years I was largely out-of-touch with Ernest. It was with pleasure and joy when I learned that he had married Ruth Erickson Krueger.

After T. K. 's death Ruth had gone back to Washington to be with old friends who wanted her with them. Ernest learned of T.K.'s death, and that Ruth had left Lakewood to go to Washington. He took a leave of absence, followed her there and wooed and married her — the culmination of years of loving her from great distance. Ruth also truly loved Ernest; her memories of the two at the Highland Ranch came back to her. She was so in love that she cast aside and lost the widows' pension she was receiving in order to marry him. They had a loving twelve years together, returning to their roots in Ouray. Ruth purchased a century-old miners house high on the amphitheater hillside; Ernest rebuilt this into a home which

This photograph of the author and his family shows the two seated surrey they rented to visit the Ericksons. The young colt stands right alongside his mother.
— AUTHOR'S FAMILY COLLECTION

became a center for music lovers and those with musical ability. Ernest just spent his time loving Ruth. When Ernest lived with us he used to say he was tone deaf, and he declined to go to concerts. Instead he would stay at home and draft plans for mining his "Miller's Millions." After he and Ruth were married I was amazed to see him sit at home, giving full attention to Ruth, and thoroughly enjoying her viola playing. It seemed obvious that it wasn't the music that was attractive, it was the musician.

After Ernest's death, Ruth pulled herself together and immersed herself in her music. She built a home in Apache Junction, Arizona where she stayed in the winter and played with the Mesa Symphony and many chamber groups. In Ouray she shrewdly acquired property and was active in the community, until nearing ninety, she moved to Florida to be nearer to her grandchildren. As I write these words I have learned that Ruth died at age ninety-five. What an amazing love story!